# The All In One Computer Programming Bible

Beginner to Intermediate Guides on Python, Computer Programming, Raspberry Pi and Black Hat Hacking!

By

## Cyber Punk Architects

information contained within this document, including, but not limited to, —errors, omissions, or inaccuracies.

# About CyberPunk Architects

Computer programming doesn't have to be complicated. When you start with the basics its actually quite simple. That is what Cyberpunk Architects are all about. We take pride in giving people the *blueprint* for everything related to computer programming and computer programming languages. We include Python programming, Raspberry Pi, SQL, Java, HTML and a lot more.

We take a sophisticated approach and teach you everything you need to know from the ground up. Starting with a strong base is the only way you will truly master the art of computer programming. We understand that it can be challenging to find the right way to learn the often complex field of programming especially for those who are not tech savvy. Our team at Cyberpunk Architects is dedicated to helping you achieve your goals when it comes to computer programming.

We are here to provide you with the *blueprint* to give you a strong foundation so you can build on that and go into any area of programming that you wish. Our architects are comprised of professionals who have been in the industry of information technology for decades and have a passion for teaching and helping others especially through our books. They are friendly, experienced, knowledgeable computer programmers who love sharing their vast knowledge with anyone who has an interest in it.

We look forward to getting a chance to work with you soon. Here at Cyberpunk Architects, you can always be sure that you are working with right people. Allow us take care of your needs for learning computer programming. If you have any questions about the services that we are providing, please do not hesitate to get in touch with us right away.

# Table of Contents

# *Chapter 1: Why Learn Computer Programming*

Computer programming is a great skill to learn how to use. Most people are worried that computer programming is going to be too hard for them to learn. They feel that unless they spend a lot of time learning the computer or having to spend years at school in order to do anything. But even as a beginner, it is easy to learn how to work with computer coding. In the following chapters, we are going to talk about some of the basic coding languages that are really popular and will help you to learn how to get started and you will be able to see how easy computer programming can be.

You don't have to do something that is too complicated when you are getting started. You won't have to know how to hack onto some of the other computer systems or create operating systems or anything like that when you are first getting started. If you want to get to that later on, it is something that you can work with, but for now, some of the basics are all that you need to get started and have a good time. Let's take a look at some of the reasons that you would want to learn how to work on computer programming before we move on to some of the best coding languages that you can use to get the most out of your new coding skills.

**Make your own programs**

One of the best options that you can do when it comes to using a new coding language is that you are able to make some of your own codes. Each of the coding languages will have their own options when it comes to what you are able to create. For example, C# is a more advanced option that can handle some of the bigger projects that you want to work on while Python is good for those who are beginners and Java and JavaScript are great for when you want to work on your own websites and the add-ons that come with them.

You will find that there are so many programs that you are able to make when it comes to a coding language and you are able to design almost anything that you would like.

One good idea to work with is to make sure that you figure out what kinds of projects that you would like to work on and then figure out what coding language that you would like to work on to make that project a reality. The only limitation is your imagination when it comes to the things that you are able to create.

## Answer questions when things go wrong

No matter what kind of computer you have, there are always times when something will go wrong. The computer could run into an issue with a new program that you are working on or it may get a virus or another issues. Sometimes the computer gets old and just needs a little bit of extra help compared to some of the others.

When these things go wrong, many times we are going to try to find a computer professional and pay them a lot of money in order to get them all fixed up. We get the problem fixed in this manner usually, but we have no idea of the type of issue that was going on or even how it was fixed in the first place. This is fine for some people, but wouldn't it be nice if we were able to understand what is going on with our computers and even how to fix them ourselves?

When you learn a bit about coding, you may be able to fix some of the issues on your own. You will be able to use some of the coding to take a look through the issue that is coming up on your screen and make some changes. You maybe will be able to figure out that the new program you installed is not the best one for your particular computer program, perhaps you placed something in the wrong order, or you can make some simple changes.

The coding that you will learn may not be able to fix all of the issues that come up, but you will find that it can make a bit difference in how well you can take care of and fix the issues on your computer.

**Learn more about computers**

Even if you don't have any ideas for programs in mind right now, it is still a great idea to work with a new coding language. You are going to be surprised by how much it is able to teach you about your own computer.

These coding languages are going to help you to manipulate and change around the things that are going on in your computer, whether you are trying to look things up or to make a new program. In this guidebook, many of the programs that we are going to do concentrate on the Hello World program to get started, so that you can get used to them and you get to see how your computer will react to each of the codes.

Many times we are going to get into a new coding language and be uncertain about what we are doing. Most of us have not spent the last many years working in computers and making them our own. But with the help of a new coding language and learning something new, we will learn so much great stuff about how our computers work.

# *Chapter 2: The C++ Programming Language*

The C++ language is another one that you may want to add into the mix when you are learning ow to work with the coding languages. It is simple to learn and you are going to love some of the results that you get. It is a bit easier to learn compared to the C# language and it provides you with many great programs that you are going to love. Before getting started, make sure to visit https://www.microsoft.com/en-us/download/details.aspx?id=5555 to get it ready for your computer. Let's take a look at some of the great things that you are able to do with this coding language.

### The Hello World Program

Now that you have had some time to set up your environment, it is time to work on your first code and learn how to write a program in this language. We are going to work on the Hello World code and see how easy it is to write out the first code inside this language. In order to get the screen to print out Hello World, you would need to type in the following:

```
#include <iostream>
using namespace std;

//main() is where program execution begins

int main()
{
        cout <<"Hello World"; //prints Hello World
        return 0;
}
```

Now that we have written out the code, we need to look at all the parts to learn what they mean. First, C++ will involve a variety of headers which are used to hold onto useful information and data for the program. The <iostream> header is the one required for this code. We then moved on to adding in the line "using namespace std". At this area, we are telling the compiler which namespace to bring up your information.

The int main() part is going to tell the program that this is the primary function where the program should start being executed and the two slashes are comments that let other programmers know what you are doing in the code without effecting how well the code works. All of this is going to come together in order to print off "Hello World" onto the screen.

**Comments in the Code**

Comments are important when working inside of the C++ coding language. These are going to help you to explain certain parts of the code to the other programmers who may be looking through the code or can even be used as a way to name your new code. If you use the right symbols inside of the comment, the compiler is just going to skip right over the comment so any comments that you write out won't mess up the code or change anything.

If you would like to write out a comment inside of your code, you would need to use the /* at the beginning of the code and then the */ at the end of the code to show the compiler that you are done writing out the comment at this point.

**C++ Variables**

When we are working inside of C++, a variable is going to give you a name for the storage of data inside of the program. Each of the variables that you have inside of the C++ program is going to have a specific type, even with this particular code that you are working on. The variable is going to also work to determine the size as well as the layout of the memory for the variable and the range of values that you can store inside of the memory.

When it comes to naming the variables, you will be able to use the underscore character, digits, and letters in order to get it named right, but you will need to make sure that the beginning is either an underscore or a letter rather than a number. There are many variables that you will be able to use, but the most common types include:

Bool: this is going to store values of false or true.
Char: this is going to usually just be one letter or number and it is considered a type of integer.
Int: this is often considered the natural size of the integer.
Void: this is the one that you will use if there is an absence of a type in your code.

You will want to declare your variables so that the compiler knows that there is one present and is able to know the type and the name before proceeding. The variable declaration will have meaning only when it is compiled because the compiler will actually need a definition of the variable when it is time to link them up. If you are using several files in order to define the variable, you will need to go through a variable declaration. The extern keyword is the best for helping to declare the variable at any place that you want in the code.

A good example of writing out a variable inside this language includes the following;

```cpp
#include <iostream>
using namespace std;

// Variable declaration:
extern int a, b;
extern int c;
extern float f;

int main () {
  // Variable definition:
  int a, b;
  int c;
  float f;

  // actual initialization
  a = 10;
  b = 20;
  c = a + b;

  cout << c << endl ;

  f = 70.0/3.0;
  cout << f << endl ;

  return 0;
}
```

# *Chapter 3: The C# Programming Language*

The first language we are going to work with is the C# programming language. This is a very popular coding language, but it is considered an intermediate one to learn. You will like that there is a lot of power that comes with this coding language and it is very easy to learn how to use and create your programs from. To get started with some of these options, make sure to visit this website to download the C# language: http://www.microsoft.com/en-us/download/details.aspx?id=7029

**What are the variables?**

When we bring up the topic of variables in our code, we are talking about the names that we give to all the data that is inside our programs; these data types are ones that we want to store for now but which we may want to manipulate a bit later on. For example, if you want to store the age of your user inside of the program, you would need to name the data, using the userAge, and then declare that this is a variable userAge with the following statement:

int userAge:

This declaration statement will be used in order to state the data type that is going with the variable and then the name as well as the data type will refer to any data that is stored inside of the variable (which depending on the code can be either some text or a string of numbers). Since we used the variable (int) for this example, the code is going to show that there will be an integer inside, which is something that works since we want to get an age, or a number. After you take the time to declare the variable of userAge, the program will save some space in the memory of your computer so that this data can be stored. You can come back and find this variable later on and access any of the data, even making some modifications, simply by using the right name later on.

**The data you will see inside of C#**

When it comes to picking out the data types, there are some variety that comes with this kind of language. Some of these we are going to talk about throughout the book because they are common and will work on many of the codes that we are trying to write. Some of the most common data types that are found in this language include:

Int: this is the one that will stand for integer. It is going to be a number of some sort, as long as it doesn't have a decimal or a fraction in it.

Char: this is the one that will stand for character. It is a single unit inside of the code and it can be used in order to store that single character. You can add together characters inside the code to get what you would like.

Bool: this one is going to stand for Boolean and it is based off the idea of being either true or false. It is often used to help out with control flow statements and will check to see whether your answer is true or false based on the conditions that you are using.

String: this is the one that is used any time that you would like to create, manipulate, or even compare different pieces of text that are inside of the code.

Another data type that you will probably utilize a lot when working in C# includes the operator. These operators are really busy in the code because they are responsible for doing so many different things. They can assign a value to whatever variable you are working on, they can compare different variables to see if they are alike or different, and they can even do some mathematical equations for you. There is just so much that the operators are going to be able to do to help you out.

Some of the different types of operators that you can work with include:

*Arithmetic Operators*

The arithmetic operators are responsible for helping you to do various mathematical equations. If you need to add a few variables together or do something else similar, these are the ones that you will need to work with. Some of the arithmetic operators that you are able to choose from include:

(+): this is the addition operator.

(-): this is the subtraction operator

(*): this is the multiplication operator

(/): this is the operator for division

(%); this is the modulo operator

(++): this is the increment operator and is used to increase the value of your operand by one.

(--): this is the decrement operator and it is used in order to decrease your operands value by one.

One thing to remember when working on your code is that you are able to use multiple of these inside of the same part. You can add together more than two numbers or you can do a combination and add together a few numbers before subtracting others and so on. You just need to remember that the order of operations is going to come into play here and the system is going to go in a certain manner in order to get the right answer. It is going to first multiply, and then divide, and then move on to addition and subtraction, going from left to right, to get the correct answer.

*Relational operators*

Next on the list is the relational operators. These are the ones that will compare whether the two operands you have are equal or not equal and then give you the right result at the end. The most common types of relational operators that you may find include:

(==): this is the equal to operator. If the two values are equal, you will get a true result.

(!-): this operator is the not equal operator.

(>): this is the greater than operator.

(<): this is the less than operator.

(<=): this is less than or equal to.

(>=): this is greater than or equal to.

When you are working on the relational operators, you are working with the Boolean data type. This means that the result you are getting will be either true or false. If the answer gives you a return of true, it means that the statement that is connected to your code is going to be executed. But if it ends up that the statement is false, the code is going to end; if you set up a conditional statement, it will be the second statement that releases if your answer returns a false.

*Logical operators*

There are several logical operators that you will be able to use inside of your C# code including;

(&&): this is the logical AND. It is only going to show up as true if both of your operands are true.

(||): this is the logical OR. This operator is going to give you true for an answer if at least one of your operands ends up being true.

(^): this is the logical exclusive OR and it will result in a true if one of your operators is true.

(!): this one will be able to reverse the value of the Boolean variable.

These are similar to the relational operator because it is also going to be seen as a Boolean answer. Your return is going to be either true or false and depending on the conditions that you set up, you will be able to get the right statements to show up on the screen.

## Working on Your First Code

Here we will need to open up the compiler for C# and get started on our very first code. Here is what we will need to write out to get that to work:

```
using System;
using System.Collections.Generic;
using SystemLinq;
using System.Text;
using System.Threading.Tasks;

namespace HelloWorld
{

        //A simple program to display the words Hello World

        class Program
        {
            static void Main(string[] args)
            {
```

```
Console.WriteLine("Hello World!");
Console.Read();
    }
  }
}
```

As you work on this code, you may see that while you are typing, there is sometimes a box that appears that will provide you with tips or other help. This is the Intellisense part that comes with the VSC compiler and it is good for beginners who need some help with the code they are writing. If you are uncertain that you are writing the code properly or you don't know what you should write out next, this is a good thing to look for. Once you have this code typed into the compiler, you can push on the Start button on your menu so that the program is executed.

If you have some trouble getting the VSC running, you will see that the compiler will provide you with the "Output Window" error. You will be able to push on the error to see what it is and make the changes that are needed before running the program.

Now, if you wrote the code properly, and the program doesn't bring up any other issues, you should have a little black window that comes up on your screen that says "Hello World" inside. When you see this and are satisfied with the work, you will can exit out of this by pressing the Enter key. And now you are done with the first program you need for C#.

# *Chapter 4: The Python Programming Language*

Python is considered one of the best coding languages if you are a beginner. It is really easy to use and can even be combined with a lot of the other coding languages if you are looking on getting started and want to add in some more power along the way. It is one of the best and has a huge support group to help you out with any of the programs that you want to create. To get the Python language on your computer, visit www.python.org/downloads

There are so many things that you are able to do in order to get a code up and running on Python. Many people may avoid using Python because they think that it is too simple or it just isn't going to get the job done. But in reality, it is simple just for the fact that even a beginner is able to learn how to use it, but that doesn't mean that you aren't able to do a lot with it. This chapter is going to take some time to look at the different commands that you can do with Python programming in order to make your programs and codes come to life.

## Variables

Variables may sound like something that is too complicated to learn, but they are basically locations in the memory that are reserved in order to store the values of your code. When you work on creating a variable, you are reserving this spot in the memory. In some cases, the data type that is in the variable will tell the interpreter to save the memory space and can even decide what you are able to store on your reserved memory.

## Assigning values to your variables

The value is going to be one of the basic things that your program will need to work with. It can be a string, such as Hi World, 3.14, which is considered a type float, or a whole number like 1, 2, and 3 which is considered an integer. Python variables will not need an explicit declaration in order to reserve the space in the memory that you need. This is something that is going to happen automatically whenever you place a value with the variable. For this to work, simply place the (=) so that the value knows where it is supposed to go.

Some examples of this include:

*X = 10            #an integer assignment*
*Pi = 3.14         #a floating point assignment*
*Y= 200            #an integer assignment*
*Empname = "Arun Baruah"         #a string assignment*

Keep in mind that when you are working on codes, you are able to leave a comment with your wok by using the # sign. This allows you to explain what is going on in the code, leave some notes, or do something else within the program. It is not going to be read by the interpreter since it is just a little note that you are leaving behind for yourself or for someone else.

The next part is going to depend on which version of Python you are using. Python 2 is fine with you writing out print and then the information you want to talk about but Python 3 is going to require you to place the parenthesis in to make it work. An example would be:

Print("y = %d" %y)
Print("x = %d" %x)

Pring("Employee Name is %s" %empname)

These would then be put through the interpreter and the outputs that you would get should be

X = 10

Y = 200

Employee Name is Arun Baruah

Now go through and put in this information to your program and see what comes up. If you didn't get the right answers like listed above, you should go and check that the work is done. This is a simple way to show what you are able to do with Python and get the answers that you need.

**Multiple Assignments**

In addition to working with the single variables that were listed above, you will also be able to work on multiple assignments. This means that you are going to be able to assign one value to several different variables at the same time. To do this, you would just need to place the equal sign between all of them to keep things organized and to tell the computer that the value is going to be with all of the variables together. You can keep them separated out if that is easier for you, but using this method is going to help you to send everything to the same memory location on the computer and will give the code a clearer look on your screen.

A good example of how to give more than one variable the same value includes:

a = b = c = 1

This is telling the code that you want all of them to be tied with the value of 1 and that all of these variables should have the same value and that you want to assign them all to the same location within your memory.

**Standard Data Types**

Another thing that you are able to work on when doing Python is the various data types. These are going to be used in your code in order to define the operations that you can do on each data type as well as explain to others the storage method that will be used for this kind of data. Python has five data types that are considered standard including:

Numbers
Dictionary
Tuple
List
String
Numbers

Number data types are the ones that will store the numeric values. They are going to be created as objects once you assign a value to them. There are also four different types of numericals that Python will support including

Complex (such as complex numbers)
Float (floating point real values
Long (long integers that can also be shown as hexadecimal and octal.)
Int (signed integers)

One thing to note is that while Python will allow you to use the lowercase l when doing the long form of a number, it is best to go with an uppercase L whenever you are using the letter. This is going to help you avoid confusion in reading the program between the l and the 1 as they look really similar. Any time that Python is displaying a long integer that has the l in it, you will see the uppercase L.

## Strings

Strings are identified in Python as a contiguous set of characters that will be shown by the use of quotations marks. Python is going to allow for either double quotes or single quotes, but you do need to keep things organized. This means that if you use a double quote at the beginning of your string, you need to end that same string with the double quote. The same goes when you are using a single quote. Both of these will mean the same thing, you just need to make sure that you are using the proper quote marks to make the code look good and to avoid confusing the Python program.

In addition to being able to print off the string that you would like, you are also able to tell the program to print just part of the string using some special characters. Let's look at some of the examples of what you are able to do with the strings, and the corresponding signs that you will use at well, to help illustrate this point.

```
str = 'Hi Python!'
print(str)      #prints complete string
print(str[0]) #prints the first character of the string
print(str[2:5])      #prints characters starting from the 3rd to the 5th
print(str[2:]) #prints string starting from the 3rd character
print(str*2)   #prints the string two times
print(str+"Guys")    #prints concatenated string
```

For the most part you are probably going to want to print out the whole string to leave a message up on your program so the first print that you do is going to be enough. But if you just want to print out Hi or some other variation of the words above, you may find that the other options are really useful. You can do any combination of these, they are just examples to help you get started!

## Lists

Lists are one of the most versatile data types that you can work on in Python. In this language, the list is going to contain different items that are either enclosed with the square brackets or separated out with commas.

They are similar to the arrays that you would see in C if you've worked with that program. The one difference that comes up with these is that the items that are in a list can be from different data types.

The values that are stored inside the list can be accessed with a slice operator as well as the [:} symbol with the indexes starting at 0 at the beginning of the list and then working down until you get to -1. The plus sign will be the concatenation operator while you can use the asterisk as the repetition operator. For some examples of what all this means and how you can use the different signs within your programming, consider some of these examples:

*list = ['mainu', 'shainu', 86, 3.14, 50.2]*
*tinylist = [123, 'arun']*
*print)list)      #prints complete list*
*print(list[0]) #prints the first element of the list*
*print(list[1:3]-      #prints elements starting from the second element and going to the third*
*print(list [2:])      #prints all of the elements of the list starting with the 3rd*

*element.*

*Print(tinylist\*2)        #prints the list twice.*

*Print(list + tinylist) #prints the concatenated lists.*

## Dictionaries

Dictionaries are another kind of tool that you can use when you are working in Python. They are similar to a hash table type and they are going to work similar to the hashes or the arrays that you can find on other programming languages like C# and Perl.

They will also consist of key value pairs and while the key can be almost any type on Python, you will notice that they are usually going to be strings or numbers. For the most part, when it comes to values, you will find that they are an arbitrary object in python.

Some examples of how this will work include the following codes:

*#dictionary stores key-value pair, later to be retrieved by the values with the keys*
*dict = {}*
*dict['mainu'] = "This is mainu"*
*dict[10] = 'This is number 10"*
*empdict = {'name': 'arun', 'code':23, 'dept': 'IT'}*

*print(dict['mainu']) #this will print the value for the 'mainu' key*
*print(dict[10])               #this will print the value for the 10 key*
*print(empdict)                #this will print the complete dictionary*
*print(empdict.keys())      #this will print out all of the keys*
*print(empdict.values())    #this will print all the values*

One thing to keep in mind is that these dictionary values are not going to be stored in an order that is sorted. They aren't going to have the concept of ordering among the elements. This does not mean that you can say that the elements are out of order, they are just going to be unordered.

**Keywords**

Most of the types of programming languages that you will deal with will have some keywords or words that are reserved as part of the language. These are words that you really shouldn't use in your code unless you absolutely can't help it.

There are 33 keywords found in the most recent version of Python and you will need to spell them properly if you want them to do the job that you lay out. The 33 keywords that you should watch out for include:

False

Class

Finally

Is

Return

None

Continue

For

Lambda

Try

True

Def

From

Nonlocal

While

And

Del

Global

Not

Yield

As

Elif

If

Or

Assert

Else

Import

Pass

Break

Except

In

Raise

Keep this list on hand if you are worried about learning the language. It will be able to help you out any time that you have issues with the interpreter about the names that you are giving the variable. You may be confused about why it is giving you some issues with the words you chose, you can go through with this list and see if you used one of the keywords inappropriately within your code.

## Statements

When you are writing your code in the Python language, you are going to be making expressions and statements to get it done. Expressions are going to be able to process the objects and you will find them embedded within your statements.

A statement is basically a unit of code that will be sent to the interpreter so that it can be executed. There are two types of statements that you can use; assignment so far and print.

You will be able to write out the statement, or multiple statements, using the Python Shell to do so interactively or with the Python script using the .py extension that we talked about later.

When you type these statements into the interactive mode, the interpreter will work to execute it, as long as everything is properly in place, and then you can see the results displayed on the screen. When there are quite a few lines that you need to write in code, it is best to use a script that has a sequence of statements. A good example of this is:

```
#All of these are statements
X = 56
Name = "Mainu"
Z = float(X)
Print(X)
Print(Name)
Print(Z)
```

**Operands and operators**

There are a lot of great symbols that are going to show up when you make a code in your Python program. It is important to understand what parts you are able to work with and what they are all going to mean. Operators are often used to mean subtraction, addition, division, and multiplication. The values of the operator will be called operands. You can use many different signs for these in order to get the values that you would like to see.

While you are using the operators and operands, you need to remember that there is going to be an order of evaluation that is followed. Think about going back to math class and how this all worked. You had to look for specific signs in order to figure out which tool you were supposed to use in order to come up with the right answer. This is the same when using these operands within your code.

When you have more than one of these operators in the expression, you will need to do the order of evaluation based on the rules of precedence. For anything that is arithmetic, Python is going to use the acronym PEMDAS which is parenthesis, exponentiation, multiplication, division, addition, and subtraction. If there are a number of these that are the same, such as two sets of numbers that need to be multiplied together, you will need to work from left to right to get the correct number.

Another important operator that you should look for is the modulus operator. This one is going to work with integers and is going to yield the remainder once the first operand has been divided by the second one.

# *Chapter 5: Working with the C Coding Language*

Working with the C language is pretty simple. You can write a code that just has one line or you can go on and write a nice long one that is going to be more complex and could run a game or some other process. While you can get more complex later on, I am going to look at some of the basics of writing inside of the C language to help you to get comfortable. A good place to start when looking for downloading the C language (and to get Visual Studio with it which is one of the best), includes: https://www.visualstudio.com/vs/

**Writing a Dummy Code**

First, let's take a look at writing out your dummy code. This isn't going to bring you an output like some of the other codes that we will discuss later on, but it will help you to get the hang of creating and saving a code in the C language so you are ready for the things we do later on.

So to start, you need to go into the Code Blocks IDE, or whichever IDE that you chose, and click on the New Button. You will want to open up an Empty File. Now you will need to type in a code into the editor so that you are able to create a code to save. I am going to keep this simple and just type in one line like the following:

main() {}

Now you will need to save the source file and you can do this by clicking on the Save button. You can either let this save on the default of your computer or you can choose the folder that you would like all of these code files to be saved on your computer; the choice is up to you, just remember where you are saving all of these so if you need to find them later.

Make sure to name the file something that you will be able to remember later on, or you will get confused as you start to add on more of these files over time. I am going to call this file "dummy.c". Once you have saved this, the source code file is created and it has been saved on your computer. Now you will click on the Build button.

You will notice that the code is not going to compile. What you are going to see is the minimum of the C program, which is also called the dummy. All of your codes in C need to have the main function because this is where the execution of the program is going to start; you will just need to put the main function inside of the curly brackets.

Since this is a dummy source code and one where we are just experimenting a little bit, I didn't have us put any code into the curly brackets. When you try to run this option, you will not get an output because nothing was placed inside. We will be able to add in different things later on and create an output based on what is inside the code. You may see a compiler warning when entering the dummy code, but this is not critical. You will just click on your Run button and then find that it is not able to give you any output.

Congratulations! You have just written your very first code using the C programming language. If you didn't get any output, you did the code right. This is just the basic form of writing a code in the C language and there is so much more that you are able to add into the code. Some of the other basic parts that you can add into your code includes:

Structure

Variables and values

Operators

Functions

Keywords

I am going to take you through how some of these work so you can learn how to make the code shine the way that you would like.

**Writing Another Code**

Now that I have had some time to explain a few of the basic parts of code writing, let's take a look at how this would work by bringing out our dummy.c program from earlier. Just open up the code from wherever you stored it before and I am going to make the main function be defined as an integer function. This basically means that it is going to return an integer value onto the operating system. We will need to do some editing in order to make this happen.

Inside of your editor, you will need to add in the keyword "int" before your "main" part to ensure that you are getting the integer output that you would like. Make sure that you place a space between both of these keywords to help the compiler to read through both of them. So to start, type out the following code:

```
int main()
{
}
```

You will notice that the code is a bit different than we originally wrote out with the first code, but putting the curly brackets in this manner is what most veteran programmers prefer to use. Now it is time to add in a statement to this main function so that it will actually show you an output. I will keep it simple and just add in the number three.

You will first need to type in the "return" and then the number three. I will write out the example of the syntax that you would use to make this happen:

```
int main()
{
        return(3);
}
```

Make sure to add in the semicolon after the statement. Save the file and then click on the Build button. As long as you type in the code like I wrote above, you shouldn't have any issues with errors or messages coming up for you. Click on the Run Button.

When using a Linux or Mac system, it is possible that you won't see any output other than the build log, and it will say that the program terminated with a status of zero. On a PC computer, the terminal window is going to show you the return value 3.

Any time that you want to add in an output to your dummy program, you need to bring in the output function. The keywords in the C language aren't going to output anything because they are just basic vocabulary, such as the words int and return. You can do this by using the "puts" command inside the program.

Let's take a look at how this is going to work when you write out some code. Make sure that the function of the "puts" is inside of parenthesis and that you place in a string of text between a double quote to make it work properly. Here is the example I am going to use:

```
int main()
{
        puts("I am the King of the C programming world");
                return 3;
}
```

When you save this source code and then click on Build, you should see a warning come up on your computer. Even if you don't see this, you need to realize that you have another step to do at this point. Before the puts function is going to work, it needs to have a definition inside, or you will find that the compiler is confused. The definition of your puts will be in the I/O header file and you need to place this into the source code with the help of the preprocessor directive.

Here is an example of how that would look inside of your code to keep things organized and to avoid errors.

```
#include<stdio.h>

int main()
{
        puts("I am the King of the C programming world");
                return 3;
}
```

This version includes the preprocessor directive along with the definition for the puts function. You can save the file and then click on the Build and Run buttons that are at the top of the editor. If everything is typed properly, you can avoid errors and in the output terminal window, the statement that you wrote out for the puts function as well as the value 3 will show up on the screen.

Learning some of the basics of writing a code in the C language can make it easier to understand what is going on. I showed you a few of the options that you have when working inside of the C language, but there is still so much more that you are able to do. Take some time to get familiar with how these codes work, play around with the IDE and the compiler, and get comfortable before moving on and learning some more complex options when writing your own code.

# Chapter 5: The JavaScript Programming Language

JavaScript is a good coding language to learn if you want to work on a website or online. This one often goes with the Java program, remember that these two are separate, in order to add some little add-ins into the whole program. It is really easy to learn and can make all the difference in how your program is going to work. Let's take a look at how the JavaScript program will work as you first get started.

**Getting Started on JavaScript**

The first thing we will need to do here is download the JavaScript language by visiting www.javascriptlint.com/download.htm. JavaScript is a versatile coding language that you are able to inject anywhere you would like in your page. As long as you have the HTML tags <script>...</script> around what you would like to insert. But in most cases, you will be recommended to place the script that you want to use in between the head sections or the <head>...</head> tags.

When the browser is taking a look at the content on the page, or the HTML on the page, it is going to just read through the whole thing like reading through a book. But when the browser program comes to the <script> tag, it will start to interpret whatever you have written between these tags and won't stop until it reaches the </script> part of the tag. This allows the program to interpret what you would like to have on the page in any location that you would like.

When working with the script tag, you will be able to give them one of two attributes including:

Language—this is the attribute that will specify what kind of scripting language you are using. The value for the JavaScript language is basically "javascript." If you are using a newer version of HTML, this is something that been phased out so you may not have to worry about it at all.

Type—this is the attribute that will indicate the scripting language that you are using and the value that you are using with it will be set to text/javascript when in the JavaScript language.

## Writing a program

At this point you may be a bit confused on what is going on and what all of these things mean. Let's take a chance to open up the html file (use the steps that were in the first chapter if you don't already have this opened up) and then we can get started at writing your first JavaScript program. To do this, just use the code that is below:

```
<!DOCTYPE html>
<html>
<head>
<meta charset- "ISO-8859-1">
<title> My First JavaScript Program </title>
</head>
<body>
     <script language = "javascript"
type = "text/javascript">
     document.write("Welcome to JavaScript First Program");
     </script>
</body>
```

*</html>*

This may seem like a lot of information to put into the code, but it is going to ensure that you are getting everything in that is needed to make a great code that others can read through. Let's separate each of the parts out to help you understand what is going on a bit better!

*Explaining the code*

In this code, the JavaScript code was inserted between the <body> ... </body> tags in the HTML. The code was first declared with the right attributes and then with using the document object you were able to write out the message that helped to welcome others on to the webpage. So when this is executed, the webpage should have the words "Welcome t JavaScript First Program" right at the top.

*Output*

When you take the HTML program that we just wrote up and try to execute it, the results that you will get would be:

Welcome to JavaScript First Program.

This is basically what you told the computer system to write so if you have put everything into their right spaces within the code that you were writing, this is the exact phrase that should show up when you are working on the code.

*Line breaks and white spaces*

When it comes to having spaces in your code, or even line breaks, you can use them as much as you would like. These can often help to clear up what you are writing and you won't have to worry about the code getting too long or too hard to read. That being said, it really doesn't matter how much, if any, space that you put into the code. The browser parser is not going to read these spaces so you can write out the code in the way that works for you.

This makes it easy for you to create the indentation, lines, and other parts that you need in order to make sense of the program, to help format it properly, and to keep it looking nice. Just because the lines and the spaces aren't recognized in JavaScript does not mean that you should completely ignore them in the process.

When you are first getting started with this language, it may be a good idea to add in a few more line breaks and indents to your code. This is going to make it a bit easier to read through and you can catch some of the mistakes a bit easier. The extra white spaces aren't going to change how the system will read through the information, but it can make it easier for you to read the code and for other beginners to know what you are trying to write out.

*Using semicolons*

For the most part, you will end all of your statements using the semi-colon when you are in JavaScript. These are optional if you are placing the statements on different lines from each other so the choice is really up to you. If you just write out the code with everything on one line as a continuous string, you will need to add in the semicolon but if you are separating out the statements as you go onto different lines, it is your choices whether you would like to use them. It is considered good programming practice to have them there regardless, but the program will work whether you place them there or not. The codes that we have in this guidebook will use the semicolons to help keep things clear.

*Case sensitivity*

You will notice that JavaScript is one of the languages that is sensitive to the cases that you are using. This means that you need to keep your use of uppercase and lowercase letters consistent throughout the program. This is true for everything that you label including identifiers, function names, variables, and keywords. For example, when you are using JavaScript, LEARN and learn will be different when the programming language is going through it.

This is important to remember when you are naming your functions and statements. If you name one of them JAVASCRIPT and then try to search for it or bring it back out by using the JavaScript word, you are going to get an error sign. You do get some say in what you name them, but try to keep all of the names for the code consistent so that you name them the same way and can easily call them back up when they are needed.

*Writing comments*

There are times when you will need to write out a comment in JavaScript. You may want to tell someone else a bit more about the program or you are interested in explaining what should be placed in each of the statements. There are a few comment styles that are followed when you are using JavaScript in your coding including:

Single lines—if your comment is just going to take over one line, you simply need to use the double slash (//) to get it started.

Multiple lines—sometimes your comments will be a bit longer and they can take over a few lines. For this you will use /* to start the comment and then */. You are able to use this on single line options as well if you are worried about formatting.

JavaScript will also recognize the HTML comment if you would like to stick with this. The HTML comment is <!--. This will be treated just like a single line comment in this language.

Closing sequence—the HTML closing sequence sign of ❼ is not going to be recognized in JavaScript. If you would like to use this sign in your code, you will need to write it like this: //❼.

When you use these options, you are telling the interpreter that it should not read the comment. You are able to put as many of these within your code as you need as long as you use the proper formatting so that the interpreter knows what you are leaving there for others and what it should leave alone. Once the comment is over, the interpreter will go back and start executing whatever else you have written in the code.

There are a lot of different times when you will need to write out a comment to help make sense of things in your code. If you want to tell someone what you are doing within the code, answer some questions, or help yourself or another coder to understand what information needs to go into the statements, these comments are great. You can add in as many of the comments as you would like, as long as you use the right signals, because the compiler will not read through them and won't try to execute them at all.

Some examples of using comments in JavaScript includes:

*<!DOCTYPE html>*
*<html>*
*<head>*
*<meta charset = "ISO-8859-1">*

```
<title>JavaScript Comments</title>
</head>
<body>
      <script type = "text/javascript">
      <!—The opening sequence single line comment.
            The closing sequence HTML comment//-->


      // This is a single line comment.
      /*
*This is a multiple line comment in JavaScript
*/
      </script>
</body>
</html>
```

*Output*

When you do the program in HTML that we listed above, the output will just be blank. This is because the whole program is listed out as a comment and the interpreter is not going to lists out the comments because it has learned to not read them after the signals that we discussed above. If you had added in some other code in there, the interpreter is only going to read that and will ignore the comments that you add into the code. You are allowed to put in as many comments as you would like, as you can see from the example above, as long as you choose the right symbols to go with it so that the interpreter does not give you an error sign.

These are just some of the basic things that you need to understand in order to get started with using JavaScript on your own. Each part can help you to write out the syntax that you want and ensures that you are getting the very most out of your written code. Take some time to experiment with the comments and some of the other aspects we have discussed to figure out how these are going to work for you.

# Chapter 6: Working with the Java Coding Language

While JavaScript is great at putting some of the add-ins into a website, the Java code is going to be much better for writing up the whole website or other applications that you want to use online. If you are looking to create your own personal or business website, you will want to learn how to work with the Java code. Let's take a look at some of the basics that come with this coding language and how to get started.

**Writing out your code in Java**

The first step that you will need to do is to download the Java coding language. You can do this by visiting https://java.com/download. Writing code can be simple inside of Java, you just need to get some experience with working inside of the system and with your text editor. To get started with your first code inside of Java, take the following steps.

Step1: to start writing a program in Java, you will first need to set up your work environment. Open up NetBeans or whichever environment you chose for working in Java and get it ready to use.

Step 2: once the environment is up, open up your text editor that you want to use. Notepad is a good selection if you have a Windows computer, but anything that is similar will work out great.

Now we are going to create the Hello World program. This is an easy program to use on any programming language that you want to work with because you will get the hang of how the syntax works and you will get the words "Hello World" to show up on your screen.

To start this, just go to your text editor, click on new file, and then save this document as "HelloWorld.java". HelloWorld is going to be the name of your class, so keep this in mind since the class name needs to be the same as the file name.

One the file is created, it is time to declare the class and the main method. The main method will be the same in terms of method declaration no matter what kind of program you are creating inside of your Java program. At this point, you should have the following syntax:

```
public class HelloWorld {

        public static void main(String[] args) {

        }

}
```

Write this part out into your text editor. Next, you will need to write out the part of the code that will tell your text editor what you would like to have printed out. For this point, you would need to type out:

System.out.println("Hello World.");

This is going to tell the system that you want to print out the phrase "Hello World" onto the screen. You can try this out and change up the message you want to use inside of the program based on what you want to program to use. With this part, there are a few things that help to make it get done the proper way so let's take a look at how these work.

System: this part is going to alert the system that it needs to do something.

Out: this is going to tell the system that you are creating an output that you want it to print on the screen.

Println: this part will stand for print line in the system. You are basically telling the system that you want to print out the statement that comes after this part.

Parentheses: there are some parentheses that are found around the "Hello World" part. These means that the code in front of it is takin gin a parameter, or the string of Hello World.

So basically this code is working to alert the system that you need it to take some actions, that you want to create an output and that you want to print out the line

"Hello World" onto your screen.

Before continuing, there are a few rules that you should follow when making these codes inside of Java. First, it is a good idea to add a semicolon at the end of the lines. This is a good programming practice and helps the text editor to print things off properly. Java is also a case sensitive language so pay attention to whether you are using upper case or lower case letters when you are writing out class names, variable names, and method names. And finally, any blocks of code that are specific to a certain loop or method will be encased with the curly brackets.

So let's put this code all together so you can place it into your text editor in the right places.

```
public class HelloWorld {
        public static void main(String[] args) {
                System.out.println("Hello World.");
        }
}
```

Once this is written into the code, it is time to save your files and then open up a command prompt, also known as a terminal, in order to compile the program. You can navigate to the folder where the HelloWorld.java is located. Type in the words javacHellWorld.java. This is going to tell your compiler that you want to compile your HelloWorld.java.

If there happen to beany errors in your code, the compiler will be able to tell you what may be wrong with your code. Otherwise, the compiler is not going to show any messages. You can then look at the directory where you store the HelloWorld.java and inside should be the HelloWorld class that we designed. This is the file that is used when you want to run your program.

Now that we have written a program, you may want to give it a try and see if this will run. Open up the terminal or the command prompt and type out java HelloWorld. This is going to tell Java that you wish to run your HelloWorld class. If everything has gone into the program properly, the statement "Hello World" will show up on the console and you have written your first code in Java!

## Expanding the Hello World Program

Working with the Hello World program was pretty simple and has given you some experience with how this program is going to work. Here we are going to take the Hello World program and extend it out a bit. In the Hello World program, we printed out a string for the user to see, but now we are going to extend out the program so that the users are able to place in their name and then it will greet them by name.

First, we will import in the scanner class. In Java, there are a few libraries that you can access, but you first need to import them. One of the libraries that we need and which holds the Scanner object is the java.util. To import this Scanner class, use the following code:

import java.util.Scanner;

This tells the program that you wish to use your Scanner object, which is inside the java.util package. Inside of the method, we will instantiate a new instance with this Scanner object. To use this Scanner class, we just need to create a new Scanner object that we are able to populate and use the methods of. To get these Scanner objects to work for us, we would need to use the following code:

Scanner userInputScanner = new Scanner(System.in);

So what does this code mean and what is it going to tell the computer to do? Here is an explanation of how the different parts move:

userInputScanner: this is the name of the Scanner object we are using. Note that this is written in what is known as the camel case; which is the conventional way of writing out your variables in Java.

the new operator will help to create a brand new instance of your object. For this instance, we created a new instance in the Scanner object with the new Scanner(System.in) part.

This new Scanner object is going to take in a parameter that will tell the object what they need scanned. The System.in is going to work for this and it tells the program that you want to scan in the input from the system, which is basically going to be the name of the user.

Now we can work on prompting the user for their input. We need to ask the user for the input so that the user has an idea that they are supposed to type something into their console. Otherwise, the program will just sit still because nothing is entered. You can accomplish this with the following code:

System.out.print("What's your name?");

The next part that you should do is ask the scanner object to take in the information that the user types and then have it store that information as a new variable. The Scanner is responsible for taking in the data that your user is typing, which should be their name at this point. To do this, use the following code:

String userInputName = userInputScanner.nextLine();

This should tell the Scanner object that you want it to read what the user inputs into the system and use that as the variable for your next part. It can now be used as the greeting that shows back to the user. Since you have the name of the user, you can write it out so that the program mentions the name while leaving another message. The next step is to write out the following code:

System.out.println("hello" + userInputName + "!");

At this point, we have been separating out the code to the different steps and discussing it, but let's put it all together to help you see how this code should be written out:

```
import java.util.Scanner;
public class HelloWorld (
        public static void main(String[] args) {
                Scanner userInputScanner = new Scanner(System.in);
                System.out.print("What's your name?");
                String userInputName = userInputScanner.nextLine():
                System.out.println("Hello" + userInputName + "!");
```

Once this code is in the system, you will be able to compile the program and run it. Go into your command prompt or the terminal window and then run the same commands that we did with the HelloWorld.java from the last section. You can compile this program by typing in javac HellWorld.java.

When you type in the HellowWorld.java, your program should ask "What's your Name?" You can go through and type in your name. Let's type in the name Jane. Once you press enter on this name, the program will print out Hello Jane and then the program is done.

While this part may take a few more lines to complete, it is still pretty basic. It took the original skills you learned with your first part and expanded it out into a code that has a few extra parts that come with it. Despite needing a few more parts, you will find that this is a basic code that adds in a bit more personalization to the codes you make.

And now you are set to start with the Java program. You already know how to do two basic codes inside of this program and as you move through the other parts, you will be able to write out some more codes to get the hang of how the text editors work inside this program. (How To Write Your First JavaScript)

# *Chapter 7: How To Use The Linux Terminal And Master Its Functions*

As I mentioned before, Linus is Unix-like computer operating system; it is developed under the version of the free and open-source software. Unix operating systems are free for distribution and development. The most important component of Linux operating system is Linux kernel. Originally Linux was developed for personal use and computers, but since then Linux has been developing many other platforms, more than any other operating system. Today Linux is the most used operating system in the world, has the largest installed base of all operating systems and is leading operating system on many servers and desktop computers. Today many smartphones run Linux components and derivatives.

The greatest example of free and open-source software is absolutely the development of Linux operating system. Source codes may be distributed and modified by anyone by the certain terms and licenses. You can use find many popular mainstream Linux versions such as Fedora, Linux Mint or Ubuntu. You have plenty options. Besides these versions, you can find for free supporting utilities, large amount of applications and software supporting Linux operating system. All of these have supporting role in distribution's intended use.

Linux is high-level assembly, and programming language freely redistributed and with easy porting to any computer platform. For this reason, Unix-like operating system Linux quickly became adopted by academic circles and institutions. Today it is widely used and distributed all over the world. Linux is the result of the project of creating Unix-like operating system with completely free software. It is opponent to the Microsoft's monopoly in the desktop computer technology. Linux today is more used in the field of embedded systems and supercomputers.

Linux is modular operating system; device drivers are integrated or added like modules while the system is running. Some of the Linux components include C standard library, widget toolkits, and software libraries. This guide will help you and guide you through the Linux terminal commands and basics. Linux Terminal is really powerful tool, and you shouldn't be afraid to use it.

Learning the Linux basics is first and crucial step into the world of hacking. In this guide, we have to cover topics such as Linux command line and Linux executing commands. These are basics when it comes to the Linux operating system. You should familiarize yourself with the Linux Terminal emulator in the first place. It will become very easy to use when we pass through the basics first. It is needless to say you have to be able to connect to the Linux server.

At the very beginning, we should distinguish what the terminal emulator is. Terminal emulator is the program allowing the usage of terminal in a graphical environment. Today many people use operating system with graphical user interface and terminal emulator is an essential feature for Linux users. Besides Linux, you can find terminal emulator program in other operating systems such as Mac OS X and Windows. Here we are going to discuss Linux Terminal emulator.

You should be familiar with the shell. When it comes to the Linux, the shell is standing for command-line interface. The shell reads and interprets commands from the user. It reads script files and tells the operating system what to do with the obtained scripts. There are many widely used shells such as C shell or Bourne shell. Every shell has its own features, but many of the shells feature some same characteristics. Each shell function in the same way of input and output direction and condition-testing. Bourne-Again shell is the default shell for almost every Linux version.

Another important thing is knowledge of command prompt. The message of the day is the first thing you will see when you log in to server. It is message containing information about the version of Linux you are currently using. After the message of the day, you will be directed into the shell prompt known as command prompt. In the command prompt, you will give directions and tasks to the server. You will see information ate the shell prompt, and these information can be modified and customized by the users. In the command prompt, you are able to manipulate the information.

You may be logged into the shell prompt as root. In the Linux operating system, the root user is the special user who is able to perform administrative tasks and functions of the operating system. Superuser account has permission to perform unrestricted commands to the server. As a superuser, you have limitless powers when it comes to the manipulating commands given to the server. You will be able to give unrestricted administrative tasks and commands.

Besides shell prompt, we should discuss executing commands as well. You give commands to the server in the shell prompt. You specify the name of the files both as script of binary program. With the operating system Linux, there are already many utilities installed previously. These utilities let you navigate through the file system, install applications and configure the system. Giving tasks and commands in the shell prompt is called the process.

By giving directions in the command prompt, you are able to install software package and navigate through the system. When you are executing the commands in the foreground, you have to wait for the process to be finished before going to the shell prompt. This default way of commands being executed is case-sensitive including all names and files, commands and options. If something is not working as planned, you should double-check the spelling and case of all your commands.

You may have problems while connecting to the Linux server, online you can find solution to the problem with the connection. In order to execute the command free of arguments and options, you just simply type name of the command and press return. Commands like this, without arguments and options, behave differently from the commands with arguments. The behavior of the outcome varies from each command.

When it comes to the commands with arguments and options, accepting arguments and options can change the overall performance of the command. Every argument specifies and directs the command in a certain way. For example, a cd is the component of the command and arguments follows the certain command. Options that follows commands are known as flags.

Options are nothing more than special arguments directed in a certain way. They also affect and modify the behavior at the command prompt space. Same as arguments, options follow the commands and can contain more than one options for the same command. Options are single-character special arguments usually having descriptive character. Both arguments and options contain additional information about the commands and about each file and script. They can be combined into certain groups of options and arguments while running commands at the command prompt.

We should pay attention to the environment variables as well. Environment variables can change behavior of the commands and the ways of the command execution. First when you log in to server, default environment valuables will be set already according to configuration files. You can see at the command prompt all environment variables sessions by running env command. After running any command, next step is looking for path entry. The path will give you all the directions about the shell looking for executable programs and scripts.

From command prompt, you can retrieve the values of environment variables just by prefixing name of the variable with $ character. By doing this, you will expand variable to its value. IF you see an empty string, you are probably trying to access variable which hasn't been set yet. In that case, you will get empty string.

Now that you are familiar with the environment variables you are able to set them. For setting environment variable you need to type variable name followed by an = sign. Finally, you should type the desired value. The original value of the variable will be overwritten if you are setting the existing environment variable and if the variable doesn't exist by doing this, it will be created. Command export allows you to export variables inherited during the process. To be more clear, you can use any script from the exported variable from current process.

When it comes to the referencing existing variables, you can always add directory at the end of the path command. You should keep in mind that modifying and adding environment variables in this particular way only sets the environment for your current session and any changes made will not be preserved for next sessions.

# *Chapter 8: How To Be Completely Anonymous Online Like The Pro's*

Being hacker means breaking into the system, being individual who is modifying valuable information and sharing it with the world without certain authorization. Hacker gets into the system by the communication networks. Hacker essentially means computer programmer who can subvert any computer security. On the other side, there are hackers hacking with malicious purpose. These people are criminals, and they are illegally accessing computer systems. I mentioned before hackers stealing and entering into banks' and companies' computer security.

Hackers use their abilities and knowledge in computer science also good purposes as well. We are going to pay attention only to ethical and moral hacking. On the other hand, there is no surprise; hackers are disreputable. We heard about many cases in the past about stealing information which resulted in many accounts being compromised and many unauthorized transfers happen. Many banks and companies were targets and hit with the hacking attack. These attacks cost huge amount of money to both banks and companies, great amount of lost resources spent on investigation, more than stolen amount.

Hackers with malicious purposes besides stealing from banks and companies, usually steal peoples' personal information, online accounts especially social accounts and other personal files and data. When it comes to the ethical and moral hacking, you should keep in mind that you are always at risk to get caught. In this chapter, we are going to see how to be completely anonymous like a professional. Of course, keep in mind only ethical and moral hacking for good purposes is desirable hacking and any other purpose will not be discussed.

There are certain strategies and techniques how to hack like a professional and not get caught. Hackers like to get through many obstacles and penetrate into the computer system, and best way to do that is to be completely anonymous. Any other way is suspicious and may be dangerous. There are many restrictions while entering the computer system. An essential thing is being anonymous online and protecting your work. Hackers have to stay anonymous and not get traced by many tricks like using stronger passwords or using two-factor authentication.

How not to be caught and stay anonymous?

1. When it comes to the tips of being completely anonymous while hacking, the most important thing you can do is try not use windows operating system. For the perfect hacking environment, you will need unix operating system which is perfect for hacking job. Getting Linux operating system and computer will be money good spent. Windows operating system is not good for hacking due to many holes that can be traced easily. These windows holes in the security may be deciding factor in spyware infecting and compromising your anonymity. You should definitely use other operating system security hardened system.

2. The second thing you should pay attention is to avoid connecting to the internet directly. You can easily be tracked through your IP address. So if you want to avoid this, you should use VPN services which stand for virtual private network. The virtual private network allows users to share and receive files and data while online through public networks like the internet. While you are online using virtual private network, you are connected as if your computer is directly connected to the private network. All of the applications you are running through a virtual private network can benefit in functionality and security. With a virtual private network, you are going to be able to surf the internet with great security and lower risk of being caught.

How does VPN help you stay anonymous?

In order to be connected to the virtual private network, you will need to connect to the proxy servers which have purpose of protecting your identity and location as well. However many sites on the internet are blocking access to the virtual private network technology in order to prevent unauthorized entering and wandering. VPN is essentially point to point connection which is using other connections and virtual tunneling protocols. Many benefits are provided by using a virtual private network for a wide-area network.

When it comes to the hacking, VPN will let you create private tunnel, anyone who is trying to trace your IP address will only see the address of the virtual private network server, and you can choose any address in the world.

Which VPN to use?

When it comes to the virtual private network services, there are plenty of options. Some of the best software for secure and private browsing the internet are ExpressVPN, NordVPN, PureVPN and all of these are free to download. You should keep in mind before downloading VPN software that not all of these are created equal. Some of the VPN software may offer you top notch services while others can play fast with your files and data. Before buying and downloading any of the VPN software keep this in mind.

3. TOR is network full of nodes which are routing your traffic. Directions of the nodes are behind and in front. Your direction onto normal internet connections is known as exit point. The most secure and the best way is to combine both virtual private network and TOR. In order to be anonymous while being connected to the internet, you should download free TOR software. TOR software is going to protect your personal data from network surveillance and help you defend against trafficking analysis. These types of network surveillance threaten all of your personal privacy and work against your freedom. TOR software will protect and secure your internet connection and prevent other people from seeing sites you are visiting. The most important thing is that TOR software is completely free for downloading

4. Another one crucial thing when it comes to the hacking is email address. You

should never use your email address while hacking. Instead of using your real email address, you should use one from the anonymous email service. Anonymous email service is letting their users send and receive emails from someone without any trace especially if you already have TOR software and virtual private network. When you go online every site is background checking your activities like google which is expecting you to share some of your personal information like email address or number.

Which email service software to get?

In order to set completely anonymous email address that can't be traced and without a connection to any server I recommend you download the software Hushmail's. Hushmail's is software very easy to use without any advertising, but it comes with the price, and on the other hand there is free version offering 25 MB of storage. If you don't want to pay extra money for the software, another great anonymous email service is software Guerilla Mail. Messages received in this mail are only temporary and will be available only for an hour.

Great way to stay anonymous and hide your email existence is website Mailinator, free and disposable. Whenever someone asks you for the email, you just make one up and sign into the Mailinator account and check received mail without leaving any traces. With the combination of the anonymous email service, TOR software and accessing connection through the virtual private network you are almost invisible to the others. By doing this, you protected your personal information and defended from the third party sites which are tracking your IP address and location every time you go online.

5. It may seem obvious, but you should never use Google while hacking. Google is constantly tracking sites that you are visiting and all of your online activities. Google is the most useful search engine, and there is certain way for you to use it without revealing your identity and personal information. You should use some of the services for preventing Google storing your IP

address, records of your searches and cookies. I recommend you to use services such as StartPage or DuckDuck go which will prevent google from remembering your online searches and history of your online activity. You will be able to search through the google without compromising your identity.

6. Last but not least thing you should keep in mind is using public wireless connection. There is huge issue when it comes to the using public WiFi. The problem is that your computer has unique address, which is going to be recorded by the router of any public location. So if your address is tracked down by the router, it will lead to your location and device. The second problem with using public Wifi is common hacking attacks. Attacking public Wifi is known as man-in-the-middle, and it will compromise your anonymity. In that case, other hacker connected to the same network connection as you will be able to track you down. These are basic tips and precautions when it comes to the anonymity while going online and staying safe and protected while hacking.

# *Chapter 9: How To Setup NMAP*

We are already halfway; now you are familiar with the basics when it comes to the hacking. We already discussed Linux Terminal and tips and precautions for you to stay completely anonymous and protect your identity while hacking. The next thing of great importance is setting up NMAP which stand for network mapper. Network Mapper is the type of security scanner which is used in order to discover any hosts and service on the devices. A computer network is filled with anonymous hosts and services, and NMAP is tracking and discovering them and putting them together by building the certain map of network. Hence the name network mapper. In order to do this network mapper is sending special packets to the different hosts which are targets in this case and then NMAP analyzes the responses from the hosts.

Network mapping software provides many great utilities such as host discovery, operating system detection, and vulnerability detection. These are all great features for probing computer network. Besides these basic features, NMAP provides many other advanced features. Network mapper tool is constantly being developed and refined by the computer science community. Firstly it started as Linux utility, but later expanding to the other platforms such as Solaris, Windows, and IRIX. Among the IT community, NMAP utility for Linux is the most popular today and closely followed by operating system Windows.

There is no surprise that network mapper is great tool when it comes to the hacking. You should keep in mind that computer network is filled with the great number of hosts and services and network mapping is a great way to discover them all. Some of the features that network mapper provides are port scanning, determining operating system, scriptable interaction with the hosts and detection of the version meaning interrogating network services. Network mapper is used when it comes to the generating traffic to the target, finding any vulnerabilities, auditing security of your computer and analyzing open ports and preparing for auditing.

Now we should see how to setup network mapper scanning. It may sound terrifying, but it is quite easy to do, and often NMAP can be installed just by doing one command. As I said, NMAP could work on many different platforms provided with both source code compilation and installation methods.

> ➢ The first logical step for you is to check if you already have network mapper installed. Many platforms already have NMAP tool installed such as Linux and BSD. To find out if you already have NMAP, you should open terminal window and execute command NMAP, and if NMAP already exists, you will see that in the output. On the other hand, if you don't have NMAP installed you will see error message. In any case, you should consider having the latest version of network mapper and upgrading it.

NMAP is running from shell prompt. This is letting users to quickly execute the commands without wandering around bunch of configuration scripts and option fields. It may be intimidating for the beginners the fact that NMAP tools have a great number of command-line options even though some of them are ignored by many users such as commands for debugging. Interpreting and executing any outcome will be easy once you figure out how the command-line works and how to pick among command-line options,

> ➢ In case you don't have NMAP already installed, you should download one from the internet. Nmap.Org is right place for downloading hence it is official source for downloading. You can download from the Nmap.Org both source codes and binaries. Source codes will come in the shape of compressed tar files and binaries are available for many platforms including Linux and Windows.

> ➢ After you downloaded source codes and binaries from the Nmap.Org, you may be intimidated by the verifying the integrity of the maps downloaded. Many of the popular packages of the maps such as OpenSSH, Libpcap or

Fragrouter may be easily infected with the great number of malicious trojans. The Same thing can happen to the software distribution sites such as SourceForge and Free Software Foundation. You should be careful not to download infected files.

➤ When it comes to the verifying NMAP tools, you should consult the PGP signatures that come together with the NMAP version you downloaded. When you download NMAP, you will get both PGP signatures and cryptographic hashes. You can find both in the NMAP signatures directory. The most secure way of verification of the NMAP is PSG signatures which came with the tool. Of course, you will need NMAP special signing key because NMAP versions are signed with these special keys. In order to get one visit on of the popular key servers. Once you get the special signing key, you will import it through the command, and you are only doing this once. By doing this, you are verifying all of your future releases.

It is easy when it comes to the verification with the proper signature key, and it takes single command. Besides signature keys, there are other options for verifying the NMAP like MD5 and SHA1 hashes if you are more into casual validation. But be careful, hashes from third party sites may easily be infected and corrupted. Once you verify NMAP, you can build the network of the hosts and servers from the source code.

# *Chapter 10: How To Keep Yourself Safe From Being Hacked*

In this last chapter, we should discuss how to stay safe and not get hacked. Hackers can break into your personal computer network if you are not careful. They can steal your personal information. You should be careful when it comes to your digital life and take some precautions before going online and compromising yourself to the world. You should keep in mind that professional hackers can have bad purposes, can steal your bank accounts, your personal emails, and social media accounts as well. Keeping yourself from being hacked is of great importance for safe and protected digital life.

> ### ➤ **Be Careful about what you Share Online**

First and the most important thing is to be careful what you share online. Posting online info which is usually asked as security questions are not good idea. All of this information can be used by hackers to break into your personal accounts. Hackers are able to steal millions of password and personal files, causing blackouts. These tips are of great importance for not letting that happen to you.

> ### ➤ **Setting Strong and Unique Passwords**

You should always use strong and unique password. By adding extra level of protection known as two-factor authentication, you are making yourself more protected. By enabling two-factor, you are going to need something more besides password to log into your account. Often it is numerical code which is sent to your cellphone.

> ### ➤ **Download a Password Manager Tool**

Before going online, I recommend you to download a password manager tool, which is going to save all of your passwords. I recommend you to download Dashlane or 1Password.

### ➢ Use LittleSnitch

I previously mentioned you should use virtual private network that will prevent intruders from entering into your personal network by routing the internet traffic. Another great software for staying safe while being connected to the network is LittleSnitch which monitors all of your outgoing connections. It will alert you whenever computer is trying to send files to the unknown server. Your laptop should be using full disk encryption, if not you should turn it on.

### ➢ Don't Underestimate the Importance of Antivirus Programs

You should keep in mind the importance of antivirus programs. And yes, it is true that antivirus are basically full of security holes, but still having an antivirus program installed is a good idea for staying protected from trojans. Besides using antiviruses, I recommend using simple security plugins such as adblockers.

### ➢ Stop Using Flash

If you are using flash, you should know that flash is the most insecure software with a great number of security holes perfect for hackers.

### ➢ Backup Your Files Regularly

Finally, yet importantly, the last recommendation is to back up your files regularly. You should back up your files usually when you are disconnected from the network. You should use external hard disk in case you get ransomware.

You should never underestimate potential danger and threat. Hackers are always lurking new victims, take these precautions for staying safe and protected while being online. These tips can be life changing when it comes to the digital life and online freedom.

# *Chapter 11: Which Tools The Hackers Use To Crack Passwords*

You already know who is a hacker. Hackers are using their knowledge and abilities to break into the system, to access the information and modify and create something completely new. Now it is time to see which tools the hackers use in order to break into system and to crack passwords. The first and most important thing is as I mentioned before is operating system Linux which will give you complete power when it comes to using hacking tools of any kind.

There are many different types of tools for hacking, depending on the purpose and knowledge of the users. Keep in mind what type of the hacking and for which purpose you are going to do. Depending on your personal interest you may need tools for firewalls, intrusion detection systems, rootkit detectors, packet crafting tools, wireless hacking or vulnerability exploitation tools. All of these tools come bundled with Linux, so I recommend Linux appropriate toolbox.

I already mentioned network mapper as a very useful hacking tool for discovering and mapping network hosts. When it comes to the cracking password, there is a great number of tools and software of great importance for the hackers.

There are many ways of cracking password depending on the tool used.

Most common ways include cracking passwords:

- with the help of brute forcing
- by using dictionary attacks cracking encrypted passwords
- with the hashes cracking windows passwords
- by analyzing wireless packets cracking of WEP or WPA passwords
- by identifying different kinds of injections and scripts and discovering hidden scripts and resources.

Here is the list of cracking password tools I would recommend.

## 1. Aircrack-ng:

Aircrack-ng is really powerful cracking tool which includes analysis tool, detectors, and WPA crackers. Among these utilities, it also includes a great number of analysis tools for wireless LAN. It is working for cracking passwords with a wireless network interface. The wireless network interface has the controller which drivers support raw mode of monitoring and can take up a great traffic. The most important thing is that this tool is completely free to download and can work on any platforms including OSX, OpenBSD, and Linux. This tool is perfect for cracking password due to its work in the field of the WiFi security. This tool focuses on the monitoring and capturing packets and exporting it to files which will be processed by the third party tools.

## 2. Crowbar

This is the second great tool for cracking password used by many hackers. Crowbar is one of the most powerful brute force cracking tools. When you are using Crowbar, you have opportunity to be in the control of things submitted to web servers. Crowbar is not identifying positive responses, but it is comparing content of the responses with the baseline. Crowbar is completely free for downloading and works only with Linux operating system. Crowbar is powerful tool when it comes to the supporting role and is used during penetration tests.

## 3. John The Ripper

It is s the most popular password cracking tool. It is really powerful and highly effective when it comes to the cracking, and that is why John The Ripper is the part of the huge family of hacking tools Rapid7. In the field of the cryptographic system, hackers are trying to find any vulnerabilities in the security network. Cracking password means recovering password from the data previously stored by the computer system or network. One of the most popular ways of cracking a password is known as brute-force attack in which computer simply guesses and hash the passwords. If you want to be real professional in the hacking world, you should get to know more about cryptographic science. John The Ripper can be downloaded for free online, and there is also pro version which you can buy. For cracking a password, this commercial version will be enough providing you great performance and speed. Originally John The Ripper was developed only for Unix-like operating systems, but today it can work on different platforms. This tool is the best option when it comes to the only cracking passwords.

### 4. Medusa

I can't discuss hacking tools and not to mention another great hacking tool Medusa. Medusa is also brute force tool providing users with excellent performance. The biggest advantage of this tools is thread-based testing allowing you to fight against multiple hosts and users. Medusa is developed in modular design, with great features like flexible user input and it is completely free to download. Medusa is running on Linux and MAC OS X operating systems. This tool can perform attacks with great speed against a large number of protocols such as HTTP, telnet, and databases.

Besides these tools for cracking a password, I warmly recommend RainbowCrack, SolarWinds and THC Hydra.

# *Chapter 12: How To Setup Your New Hacking Environment*

It is impossible to learn everything about hacking; there is huge amount of information on the computers. People usually tend to specialize in one specific field when it comes to hacking such as software development, computer security or networking. It is a bit early for you as a beginner to think about specializing in any of these fields. You should first learn basic techniques and strategies when it comes to hacking. Later in future, you will have clearer mind about your possibilities.

Discovering and knowing what is going on inside the computer system is an essential thing, this is common goal of all hackers. By knowing what is going on inside the system, you will be able to manipulate and modify information for better. You are going to create something completely new that fits your needs. Learning about hacking is gaining access into powerful system of information and technology.

Knowledge will always be the most powerful thing, and power has been used both in good and wrong things. We will just focus on knowledge for moral and ethical purposes that benefit many people.

Here are the steps you should take to get started:

1. You have already taken the first step into the world of hacking by showing an interest and curiosity to learn about hacking.
2. Like I mentioned before, the second step is knowing the basics of programming languages. Programming skills and techniques are going to be the most valuable you have for hacking. A programming language is designed to give instructions to the machines, especially computers. With the programming languages, you

can create different programs and control the behavior of the computer. You should start with something simple like creative website or create application for smartphone.

Where and which programming languages to learn?

On the internet, there are many great tutorials about using programming languages. You can watch video tutorial as well. You shouldn't forget about library. There you can find tons of books about programming and networking. Besides video tutorials and books, there are plenty sites on the internet with step by step guides about programming.

- Java is one of the longest influential programming languages, great for beginners. It lets you think like real hacker, to think logically. Besides Java I mentioned before Python, it is open and free to use. It will teach you really useful strategies, modularity, and indentation.

3. For the perfect hacking environment, you will need certain devices. Like I said before you have to be able to be online and have point to point protocol. If you don't have one you should contact your internet provider, but don't worry, almost every DLS internet connection has PPP. Other important things are you should have some knowledge about network ports, common network protocols, HTTP and you should know how each of these things works.

4. You will need operating system that is convenient for programming. Unix operating system is perfect and suitable for hackers all over the world. Unix operating system can develop and create software that can be run on other systems as well. You can use a great number of software tools. Unix consists of many great utilities such as a master program kernel. Unix emerged as

important learning and teaching tools when it comes to computer technology.

- Besides unix operating system, you will need shell account. A shell account is user account that runs on the remote server under the Unix operating system. It gives you access to a shell via different kinds of protocols. Shell accounts have been used for file storage, software development or web space.

- You will also need a Unix box. It is a computer that runs any of the several Unix operating systems like Linux. This term Unix box came in order to distinguish Unix operating system and more common Windows operating system. Unix operating system and Unix computer are able to differentiate many different servers quickly. Unix computers are perfect for security administration as well as for hacking. The most important thing is that most internet websites are running Unix operating system.

- In order to obtain Unix operating system, you will have to buy one or get free versions. I recommend Linux operating system or BSD. Linux is more suitable for beginners because it is easy to use, so you should consider buying Linux first. You can buy Linux set online from many different sites. There are many free versions of Linux; you will just need to find someone with this operating system to burn it for your personal use. Don't worry, Linux is free for distribution, and it's not illegal to makes copies.

- When it comes to installing Linux operating system, don't worry, it is quite easy. You can find complete guides and video tutorials on the internet with the installation instructions. Just type into search engine Linux installation, you will get all of the information that you need.

**Reminder:** In order to hack and manipulate the software, you have to be able to be online using Linux operating system. Like I mentioned before, you need point to point protocol internet connection. Almost all of the DLS connections are point to point protocol, but on the other hand, dial-up is not PPP. If you have DLS connection, you are lucky, and there is no need to worry about anything. You are ready for some hacking.

5. After you get these stuff, it is time to pick books about Linux operating system or any other operating system you may be using. I recommend you books with step by step guides for beginners. Your local library has plenty of books about computer technology; it won't be a problem finding any particular one you need. For me personally, the best book about Linux is Running Linux written by Matt Welsh. It is really for beginners in computer technology. If you are maybe using other Unix versions of operating system, I warmly recommend any book from O'Reilly Collection. I find them perfect for beginners.

You have to keep in mind constantly that hacking is hard work, constant learning about information and computer science in different and intriguing ways. You just made your first step; you are intrigued by hacking world, you want to know about manipulating software, creating something completely new from information you get. That is the most important step, wanting to know more. You should keep in mind that hacking is huge devotion, you will need to expand your limits and knowledge. The most important thing is learning, so you have to read a lot about information and computer technology, search online for your many questions, visit forums about hacking. After setting up perfect environment for hacking, we should start with basics.

# *Chapter 13: TOR And The DarkNet*

I already mentioned TOR and some of its features which are very powerful software when it comes to the staying anonymous while hacking and being online. TOR is software that enables users anonymous communication by directing traffic on the internet through worldwide and free networks which are consisting of more thousands of relays all over the world. TOR is concealing your location from anyone online including all kinds of network surveillance and analysis of network traffic. By using TOR, you are making it harder for the internet activity to be traced back to you while you are online. You are preventing from being traced and hiding all of your instant messages, online posts and any visit to the web sites. TOR is originally developed in order to protect personal information, to give more freedom to the users and protect them while being online.

TOR is developed by encryption of the communication stack, nested like layers of the onion. It is working by encrypting a huge number of files including IP addresses multiple times and sending it to the virtual circuit. After the encryption is done and the innermost part of the encryption is sent to the final destination without revealing and knowing the source of the IP address. This is possible due to routing in the communication, and the IP address is more concealing by the hop in the TOR circuit. This method eliminates any way of communication peers being traced back to the user. Since network surveillance relies upon determining and discovering users destination and source, by using TOR software you will prevent revealing your identity and location to the network surveillance and be free from traffic analysis.

Beside Tor software the other important compound when it comes to the hacking world is DarkNet. DarkNet is special type of network, overlay networking allowing its users to access it only with special software and configuration. To enter into DarkNet network, you will also need specific authorization. DarkNet network is usually using non-standards protocols of communication and specific ports for accessing. There are two types of DarkNet networks. First one is friend –to-friend and privacy networks. A friend-to-friend network is usually used for file sharing, and TOR is the second one used as strictly privacy network.

You shouldn't mix DarkNet with the deep web. The deep web is the term referring to the all hidden parts of the internet which can't be accessed by any search engine such as Google and Yahoo. Some of the experts believe that content of the deep web is much bigger than the surface web. In fact, the deep web doesn't contain anything sinister but contain large databases and libraries which can be accessed only by members. Some of the search engines of deep web are FreeNet and TorSearch. DarkNet is just small part of the much bigger is known as for anonymous internet.

When you are surfing through DarkNet, both web surfers and publishers are completely anonymous. You will achieve anonymous communication using TOR software. When you are connected to the regular internet network, your computer accesses host server of the site you are visiting, but with the TOR software that link is broken. Your communication will be registered on the network, but TOR will prevent transport mediums from knowing who is doing communication. TOR as a part of DarkNet utility is perfect for anonymous communication and online freedom, running on most operating systems.

The DarkNet was originally developed for the military and government, and today they are mostly using the benefits of the DarkNet. Regular internet connection and network can easily discover your location, and this is the main reason for using DarkNet. It is also popular among journalists, politicians, activists and revolutionaries. Accessing the hidden contents of the internet is really easy. Like I said before, installing TOR browser will let you enter the DarkNet. Besides Tor, you can install The FreeNet project for accessing hidden contents on the internet and allows you in creating private networks, unlike TOR. There is another privacy network I2P which stands for the invisible internet project.

For the absolute anonymity, you should use TOR or any other privacy network together with VPN and nobody will be able to see your online activities. There is no wonder why these software for privacy are really popular today. You are never too protected. You should always keep in mind that all of the search engines you are using are tracking and remembering all of your activities while being connected to the network. Surfing through the DarkNet with TOR software you are making great steps in staying anonymous and protecting your personal information.

# *Chapter 14: How You Can Use Multiple Tools To Gather Information With Wireless Hacking*

While cracking wireless networks, hackers are attacking and defeating devices responsible for security of the network. WLANs is wireless local-area network known as WiFi. WLANs are extremely vulnerable due to the security holes. Wireless hacking is direct attract and intrusion, and there are two main problems when it comes to the wireless security. The first problem is due to the weak configuration and secondly is due to weak encryption.

You should keep in mind that hacking attack is hard job, step by step procedure. Hackers are using many techniques and strategies in order to get full access. You will need to know many combinations and methods in order to break into the security through security holes. Every wireless network is potential hole as well as wired network. Real hackers must rely on their knowledge in computer science, physical skills, social engineering and any other work that involves interaction between people.

When it comes to the wireless hacking, there are plenty of options available. Here is the list of options:

1. **Aircrack:** It is not only one of the most powerful tools; it is also one of the most popular ones for wireless hacking. Aircrack is developed for using the best algorithms in order to recover passwords by discovering and tracking down packets. Once the packet is captured Aircrack will try to recover the password. In order to attack with greater speed, it implements standard FMS attack with better optimization. There are great online video tutorials how to use Aircrack tool, and it is running on the Linux operating system. If you are using Aircrack on the Linux, it will require more knowledge of Linux.

2. **Airsnort:** It is another great and powerful tool for wireless hacking besides

Aircrack. Airsnort is a powerful tool used for decrypting any WEP wireless network encryption. The best thing is that Airsnort is completely free to download and is running both on Linux and Windows operating systems. Airsnort works in the way of monitoring computing keys and transmissions when it has enough packets previously received. Due to its simple use, this tool is perfect for beginners.

3. **Kismet:** It is another great tool used by a great number of people for wireless hacking. This one is the wireless network sniffer. Kismet is working with any wireless card and supports rfmon mode as well. Kismet is working by collecting and receiving packets passively and identifying hidden networks. You can download it for free, and it is available for many platforms including Linux, OSX, and BSD.

4. **NetStumbler**: It is wireless hacking tool used worldwide by a huge number of people. NetStumbler is running only on the Windows operating system and can be downloaded for free. There is also mini version of NetStumbler available called MiniStumbler. This tool is mainly developed for wardriving and discovering unauthorized access points. There is great disadvantage when it comes to this tool. It can easily detect by the most intrusion systems which are available today. Besides this, the tool is working poorly running on the 64bit Windows operating system. NetStumbler is working by actively collecting useful information from the network.

5. **inSSIDer:** It is one great and popular wireless scanner for Windows operating system. This tool was originally free to download but became premium, so you will have to pay in order to get inSSIDer tool. Among many tasks that this tool can perform the most important are finding open wireless access points and saving logs from by the GPS.

6. **WireShark:** It is really powerful tool used as network analyzer. With WireShark, you will be able to see what is happening in your personal network. With this tool, you can easily live capture and analyze any packets.

You can check a large number of data fast and at micro-mode. It is working on many platforms including Solaris, Windows, FreeBSD, Linux and many other. In order to use WireShark, you have to be familiar with network protocols.

7. **coWPAtty:** It is a perfect tool when it comes to the automated dictionary attacking. It is running only on the Linux operating system. With the command line interface containing a word lists with the passwords for executing the attack. This tool is perfect for the beginners, but disadvantage is that tool is slow in the process. Dictionary is used for cracking passwords, cracking the each word that is contained in the dictionary.

8. **Airjack:** It is wireless cracking tool with wide range of people using it. Airjack is running as packet injection tool, hence the name Airjack. This tool is making network go down by injecting packets.

Other than the tools, I mentioned here, and I also recommend you other tools such as WepAttack, OmniPeek, and CloudCracker.

# *Chapter 15: How to hack something or someone? (Laying down important ground rules)*

Now, when it comes to computer hacking, there is a huge amount of things which need to be taken into perfect consideration. This is something that a lot of people are interested in. With this in mind, it's worth noting that ethical hacking is becoming something more and more popular as people begin to understand the need of being properly adequate to responding to cyber criminals. Of course, we won't go in-depth in the way of becoming a criminal as this is completely out of line. Instead, we will lay down basic and advanced knowledge on hacking from an ethical standpoint. Malicious hacking is illegal, and as such, we won't provide knowledge or help to someone whose intentions are to break the law.

The following will provide you with precise and significant knowledge so that you will be capable of identifying and reacting to issues.

**What is ethical hacking?**

This is a relatively modern and particularly new field and terms which are used in order to describe an individual or a company who is using hacking techniques in order to identify potential threats on a network or a computer. The ethical hacker is going to attempt to bypass the security of the system, and he is going to search for any weak points that could be potentially taken advantage of. This information is then summarized in a report which is going to be used by the organization or the individual to strengthen the securities and ensure that these weak points are taken care of. The idea is to minimize or, ideally, to eliminate the off-chance of potential attacks.

## What constitutes it?

Of course, it's also important for the hacking processed to be deemed ethical. In order for this to happen, there are a few different things that you need to abide by.
1. You need to have an expressed written permission by the organization owning the network. Your intention should be to attempt to identify risks and help fix them.

2. You need to respect and acknowledge the privacy of the individual or the company.

3. You need to close out your work without leaving any breaches for someone to exploit at a further period. This is particularly critical.

4. You let the leading software developer or the hardware manufacturer know that there are security vulnerabilities that you have pinpointed in their software.

The truth is that this particular term "ethical hacker" has received a tremendous amount of criticism throughout time. Hacking is hacking, regardless of the sugarcoating you put around it. However, it's also quintessential to understand that when you work with a Certified Ethical Hacker or a company with the necessary licenses and authorities, there is no significant need to worry about anything. The truth is that in the majority of the situations those entities would also use as a link between judicial authorities and police and investigation task forces, working as IT expert witnesses. At the same time, you should understand that the certification for ethical hacking is issued by the International Council of E-Commerce Consultants. There are exams which need to be passed, and it's extremely thorough.

Before we proceed further with the regular processes which are involved in the check-up conducted by ethical hackers, we would also want to let you know that they've managed to prevent a staggering amount of attacks. As a matter of fact, cyber security is mainly taken seriously because of the widely public campaigns which are being given towards corporations of the kind.

Now, in order for you to understand how the entire flow goes and to potentially gain any serious hacking insights, we will go through what ethical hackers do. After that, we will explain a few comprehensive ways for you to truly hack some stuff using contemporary approaches.

### How to actually protect yourself?

Now, as a business owner, you have the ultimate responsibility to ensure that your business's operations run smoothly and that you've mitigated all the risks possible. In other words, you need to make sure that you do everything that's within your hands to prevent potential lawsuits or other harmful conducts. If you are running a business which is somehow related to the internet, you also need to make sure that you don't get hacked.

With this in mind, the sad truth is that a lot of small business owners fail to take this into account. A digital security survey which was conducted back in 2012 by Symantec revealed that approximately 83% of the small businesses had absolutely no formal cyber security plan put in motion. What is more, a whopping 69% of the companies reported that not only didn't they have a formal plan – they also didn't have an informal one. This means that they are either completely unaware of the fact that the internet is a dangerous place or that they neglect the threats. In both cases, the consequences could be devastating.

The main reason for this is because the majority of the companies tend to believe that hackers, data breaches as well as lawsuits tend to represent a small percentage of isolated incidents. This is something that they couldn't be more wrong about. Cyber-attacks cost a staggering amount of money for business. This is something that you should be thoroughly aware of. However, all of this doesn't mean that it needs to happen to you. In fact, there are quite a few different ways for you to protect your business online both before and after a certain attack takes place. So, with this in mind, let's go ahead and take a look at some of the things to consider.

## Protect Your Business against Cyber Attacks

Let's begin with one of the most important as well as basic aspects of online business security. The very first thing that you should understand is that protecting your information against cyber-attack isn't challenging and it could be carried out easily without additional hassle. Of course, it's true that hackers are particularly intelligent and determined, but the reports state that business owners aren't putting enough effort towards the employment of the best mechanisms against cyber-attacks as well. According to Verizon's study, an approximation of 80% of the victims of cyber-attacks was the so-called "targets of opportunity." This basically means that they were targeted mainly because they had a particularly poor security if they had any at all. So, here's what you can do about it.

1. Purchase original anti-virus software. It's impossible to highlight how important is that. Malware is usually used in the majority of information breaches. It could be planted in your PC or laptop through websites, emails, secure connections of your Wi-Fi and whatnot. In order to protect yourself from that, all you need to do is to install reliable anti-virus software. It really doesn't take an IT guru to do this – you can handle it on your own.

2. Encrypt information which is important. Sensitive information such as bank accounts or details about the employees should definitely be encrypted. This is the information that hackers are usually looking for. Data encryption should definitely

be used for your cloud-based services as well as for the email platforms that you use.

3. Educate your employees. The truth is that the majority of attacks would tend to happen because of shady connections to different Wi-Fi networks. Make sure that your employees realize the threat and prevent them from doing so. It is usually advisable for you to use a local cable connection as it's hard to penetrate, but if you do use Wi-Fi, you should disable the SSID broadcasting function and avoid using WEP networks.

4. Secure your hardware. Just make sure that your hardware is safely stored. Basic security measures are more than enough – locked rooms or CCTV – or both.

**Hire an Expert**

This is absolutely important. There are a lot of major corporations which have specialized in different aspects of cyber security. From comprehensive penetration testing to overall check-ups, companies of the kind are going to provide you with massive value.

What the majority of business owners tend to forget is that they could also be breaching intellectual property of someone else. An expert outside audit could help you identify weak points and make sure that everything is handled perfectly and as per the current legislative standards.

Even if there are no pending claims against your company, this doesn't mean that there won't be any for the future. Making sure that you are legally protected is also something that you need to take into account. As we mentioned above, the Internet is a particularly vast area, and you need to ensure that you are perfectly secured by all possible means. Hackers are a threat but so are pending lawsuits.

# *Chapter 16: The Most Dangerous Cyber Security Threats In 2018 – An In-Depth Look*

Now, vendors, as well as malicious wrongdoers, are constantly joined right at the more advanced security companies who would usually race to take action against the latest, most advanced threats. However, attackers seem to be capable of circumventing these particular defenses in the majority of the cases. A lot of the threats became apparent lately, but they have swelled with absolutely no obvious end anytime soon. Below, we've listed a few of the most dangerous and considerably new cyber security threats for 2017. Let's have a closer look.

## 1. Ransom ware

This is without a doubt the top of the notch in terms of contemporary hacking. It's an emerging trend which has already taken millions in ransom cash. This is actively holding the valuable information of a company or organization to ransom it for cash. The unfortunate thing is that these attacks had a significant impact on companies as well as individuals back in 2016. According to a legit report from Sonic Wall, the attempts managed to swallow an approximation of 3.8 million in 2015. However, this number expanded tremendously in 2016, reaching up to 638 million and about $209 million had been already paid out in the quarter of 2017 alone. This is a staggering amount of unmatched money, unknown for any other cyber threats.

This is definitely a significant worry for almost all organizations. However, when it comes to the particular cases, the targets of hackers are usually utilities as well as hospitals, mainly because the information there is absolutely critical for the usual mundane operations. Even though the majority of the security experts recommend doing anything but actually paying the demanded ransom, it's quite easy to understand why people would prefer to do it. Of course, you have to understand that hackers are considerate enough to make sure that the requested ransom is just as much so that the company or organization can afford it.

Now, from the technical perspective, the most common type of this attack is called "Locky," and it would most commonly arrive as a basic word document. It's going to ask the user, regardless of his kind, to enable certain macros. Once this is done, the file is going to run an automatic downloader right in the background, and it's going to install the ransom ware software. This is going to scramble the data on every single available drive, and it would most typically demand payment in bitcoins.

The worst thing about this is that there is nothing that you could do once the program is delivered. As unfortunate as it may sound, there is no effective solution for after the fact. The advice here is to make sure that you have all of your information backed up on solid drives and exterior devices.

## 2. IoT Botnet Traffic

This is another major concern that a lot of organizations are worried of. Experts believe more than 8 million devices so to speak, to be simultaneously connected to the internet throughout this year. This is going to provide a wide leeway for one of the most dangerous threats on the Internet – DDoS – distributed denial of service. Basically, this tremendous amount of connectivity is going to ensure a scale which has never been seen before.

A quick example of the gravity of this issue was a happening at the end of 2016. An extensive DDoS attack was directed to the DNS provider Dyn. It was done using something which was called the Mirai botnet. It was quickly launched from an unimaginable number of IoT devices, likely at a Dyn customer. As a result of the attack, entire structures of particularly secure and popular internet services were taken down. Some of the affected names on the Internet include Github, Twitter as well as the storage service called Box and even the PlayStation Network.

What this showed was that a lot of the service providers were actually far from being prepared and equipped for an attack with this scope. Researchers also reported that they noted IoT botnets to recruit other botnets before the attack actually took place. Even though businesses are starting to consider the actual threat of this gravity, the code for the Mirai went public, and this is one of the most significant catastrophes that we've witnessed in the world of online security.

## 3. Spearphishing and whaling

Nope, these aren't a part of your Sunday lazy day routine. The truth is that phishing attacks have been a well-established threat for a considerable amount of time. However, they are now more targeted as well as sophisticated than they have ever been before.

What you need to understand and you probably do is that this is the process of sending a fraudulent email from a company which is regularly trusted in order to target an individual. The intention is most usually to scam the person out of his hard earned money. Whaling refers to the same process, but it usually involves a high-worth individual, who is often within the organization itself in order to get them to send money to an account which is fraudulent. The FBI also has a name for these – email compromise scams. There are quite a lot of examples of companies that have fallen victim to this particular process.

For instance, a toymaker Mattel's finance executive managed to sign off on a $3 million transaction with Chinese Bank of Wenzhou as he thought it was a legitimate request. It's obvious that some of those attacks as incredibly large scale. Recent research from Proofpoint – social media phishing attacks managed to grow by 500 percent in volume from the start of 2016. This is significant, and it's attesting to the tremendous dangers which stem from those cyber-attacks. (Vatu)

## 4. Machine-Learning Enabled Attacks

Now, the truth is that artificial intelligence in certain extents is getting more and more popular. What is more a lot of organizations and large companies as well as individuals use it in order to enhance their skills? Security reports as of late indicate machine learning is without a doubt going to be particularly useful and cherished in evolving social engineering attacks when you consider the overall rate of the development that AI is currently at.

However, by combining publicly available information with complicated analysis tools as well as other capabilities, Intel Security believes that it's likely to be possible to pick up different targets a lot more precisely with a significant level of success.

In the report, it's noted that the machine learning tools are actually forcing different multipliers for those who are actively involved in different security roles. Of course, it would be generally negligent to assume cyber criminals are not adopting these particularly powerful tools.

As you can see, it's safe to say that the devastating threats for our online security are rising and increasing as we speak. Hackers are finding more and more ways actually to go ahead and handle and circumvent securities. This is why it's particularly important to ensure that everything is handled as per the highest industry standards.

Now, before we go in depth into how to protect yourself and what kind of services can you expect from cyber security companies, let's further our hacking knowledge a bit.

# *Chapter 17: Cybersecurity and the procedures it entails*

**What is Cyber Security and Why is it Important?**

It's important to understand that the world is shifting in the blink of an eye. We are living on the verge of a technological revolution, and the truth is that technology has a greater than average involvement in our everyday life. However, it doesn't stop there. Technology is an important part of every country, and it's one of the most crucial things that define whether or not the country is advanced. Technology drives success, and it's nothing without the power of Internet. And this is where the trouble presents itself. The Internet is the worldwide web which is used to transfer and access information throughout the entire world. It's also something that we use without thinking twice about it. Well, that's the thing – Internet can also pose a threat. This is why you have to understand what cyber security is and why is it so important.

**A Modest Comparison**

In order to understand what is cyber security and why is it crucial for our countries, you should first imagine a safe. That's right - imagine a safe full of your country's money. Now, while it may appear that your money is secured by this facility, the truth is that safes get breached. The same goes for the internet. The information that our officials store on their computers could be incredibly sensible and potentially dangerous if it gets into the wrong hands. Well, the problem is that it's accessible if the computer is somehow connected to the Internet. This is what hackers are for, and that's what they do. This is also why governments spend millions of dollars in order to obtain the highest levels of cyber security – because they understand the threat.

## The Importance of Cyber Security

It's impossible to stress out how important it is that our governments are well aware of what is cyber security and how important it actually is. Preventing unwanted people from accessing information is the single, most important task of our security departments. We live in a world where information is the key to everything, including disastrous events. Imagine what kind of damage could information regarding the formulas used to create chemical weapons do if it gets into the wrong hands. All of this has to be thoroughly protected, and the way to do this is to implement through layers of cyber security and integrate them into the operating systems of the computers which are used in important departments. Keeping the information secured should be the most essential and important priority of every government as it could potentially lead to catastrophic consequences.

So, as we mentioned above, it's particularly important to ensure that you are well aware of the things which are done in order to assess the threat and to potentially prevent it. There is a whole lot of different things which need to be accounted for. In certain cases, the company who's doing the report might require or advise you to go through certain certification in order to maintain the necessary levels of security. NESA and ISO are quality certifications which exemplify this in a brilliant way.

## 1. Vulnerability Assessment

Vulnerability Assessment services determine the depth and extent of your cyber defenses by evaluating them against real world attack patterns. Consultants utilize the most in-depth assessment methodologies to simulate high-quality real world scenarios in addition to providing you with in the most appropriate remediation recommendations suitable for your business. The analysis encompasses the potential damages, business impact and the chance of such event occurring, ultimately leading you to the decision of fortifying the gaps that your security requires the most.

## 2. Penetration Testing

With Network Architecture being the backbone for every corporation nowadays, it is mandatory that its security is not overlooked and regularly maintained. New attack methods and vectors are being introduced daily, which might leave your organization vulnerable to the ever-changing world of hacking, and experts are more than welcome to help you tackle the challenge of securing your information. Companies can provide you with the insight you require in order to maintain a safe and satisfying work
environment.

In order to provide a comprehensive Penetration Test, consultants utilize real-world exploitation techniques to find any security loopholes within your Cyber Security perimeter. Experts utilize advanced tactics to determine whether your important assets are at risk and can be exfiltrated by a malicious individual, thus providing you with an exact understanding of the extent of damages your company could face.

## 3. Web Application Assessment

 A Web Application Assessment performed by qualified consultants will provide you the ability to understand all vectors your Web Application needs to fortify in order to fend off malicious attacks. Assessments will identify the vulnerabilities currently being neglected by your organization and provide you with the capability to remediate them, ensuring your safe and resilient web presence.

### 4. Network Architecture Security Assessment

Bring-your-own-device (BYOD) has become a part of the regular business cycle, yet this security vector has long been overlooked. It is also a common feature to provide your employees with a corporate mobile device, but more often than not, said devices tend to fall within a gray area of IT Security, thus introducing easy access for hackers to your valuable assets. Trust our experts to assess your assets and close the security gap that portable devices might be introducing to your environment.

### 5. Mobile Device and Application Assessment

The rapid growth of IT will inevitably reach your business door, and the chances are that the business focus has left some of your Information Security Systems without the necessary operational mechanisms, policies, and procedures. It is also plausible that your IT has been handled and delivers with flying colors, yet certain policies and procedures have proven hard to enforce and track. Companies can help you assess the business procedures and policies that your corporation is currently lacking, thus actively minimizing your corporate IT risk and proactively reducing the impact of a security breach.

### 6. Information Security Management

Many organizations have recently endeavored in the field of Digital Forensics without the necessary knowledge of the requirements, infrastructure, procedures or admin necessary for the smooth operation of such vastly important aspect of Investigations. Allow forensic experts to guide you through the deep waters of Digital Forensics and Incident Response by establishing the necessary components for an effective investigative process. Companies are ready to build or optimize your entire end-to-end process, maintain a pristine forensic laboratory and fortify your capability to withstand any integrity, evidentiary or procedural challenges.

## 7. Mobile device forensics

The rapid growth in mobile device availability has led to the extensive use in both private and business engagements, thus making it one of the main areas for examination with relation to Investigations. Mobile Phones contain a plethora of recorded information that can often be of criminal nature or supportive of the malicious intent. Experts can acquire, analyze and provide you with that information, thus clearing the shroud of uncertainty pertaining to such events. Experts can utilize a range of forensic techniques and processes to ensure an in-depth analysis of the device, regardless of the make, model, and operating system.

## 8. Network Forensics

Network Forensics is the process of acquiring, analyzing and processing network events in order to estimate the surrounding details of Cyber Incidents and Security Attacks. Consultancy's experts can provide you with the means to understand the underlying details, and properly respond to network Investigations by handling the inherited difficulties of dealing with Network traffic, identifying intrusion artifacts, parsing communication vectors and extrapolating intrusion vectors.

## 9. Web and Internet Forensics

Web and Internet Investigations delve into the depths of an analyzing web and internet activity and often provide investigations with additional forensic artifacts and investigative leads. Such artifacts can be paramount to building an investigation due to the sheer volume of information available. Experts are well versed in the analysis and interpretation of such Web Artefacts and can provide you with the parsed data to unshroud any such event.

## 10. Malware analysis and reverse engineering

Malware Analysis and Reverse Engineering delves into the depths of understanding certain pieces of software and their behavior, hence providing the corporation or the individual with an understanding of the cyber-attack, its initial and post-exploitation path and fraud life cycle. Such information is critical to the detection and prevention of future cyber threats and can provide an in-depth view of the security gap and chain of events that introduced the malware to the corporation's systems.

## 11. Network Threat Assessment

A Network Threat Assessment endeavors to determine the threats, vulnerabilities and potential exploitation mechanisms that can be deployed on a corporate network. This type of assessment evaluates the risk and consequences of a real-life attack with the additional recommendations and overall improvement of the associated infrastructure.

## 12. Insider Threat Assessment

An Insider Threat Assessment addresses the potential risk of trusted insiders, employees or knowledgeable personnel capturing and exfiltrating valuable corporate data. The assessment undertakes a methodological approach to your IT infrastructure's vulnerabilities, gaps within your business processes, policies and practices, and additional checks to minimize the potential compromise.

## 13. Intellectual Property Theft Assessment

Intellectual Property (IP) is, by definition, the "the product of human intelligence that has the economic value," and is nowadays a very lucrative asset that can easy be turned into a tangible source of funds. Nearly all of the current companies have

Ideas, Knowledge, and Information, that is considered sensitive and proprietary and can be considered Intellectual Property. This highly classified data is almost always made available to employees without the necessary means of control and more often than not, with virtually no protection stopping the employee from taking and selling this data to a competitor. The expert team deals with such situations on a regular basis and can aid you in the correct assessment of the volume and sensitivity of your data. Companies specialize in the analysis of such issues and are able to guide you in the depths of understanding the data, impact, and remediation required to pursue repercussions, mitigate further damages and sustain your reputation.

## Mobile Device Security – Things to Consider

A lot of small businesses fail to take into account that the protection of their internal and corporate information should always be prioritized. The reason for this is quite obvious – we live in a connected world where almost everything is accessible through the internet. And this is especially true when it comes to mobile devices. A lot of people fail to take the importance of secure apps into account, and that's why they are left with tremendous amounts of complications.

## Why is this Issue?

The main reason for which this is a significant issue is because a lot of our operations are already transferable on the mobile environment. Starting from banking and financial apps to operational necessities such as CRMs and others of the kind – these are all now available in mobile app versions. And, with this in mind, securing data has become more and more pressing.

## A Lot can be damaged

That's just it – a lot can be damaged and potentially devastated. Sensitive information of the kind can cause your irreparable enterprise issues. Securing data, therefore, has become an integral component and you most definitely need to take it into proper consideration. There are a lot of different secure apps on the market that you can take advantage of in order to protect the information stored on your mobile phone.

Mobile device security is only going to become more pressing as time passes because it's obvious that the Internet begins to have an above than average involvement in our lives. This is the main reason for which you need to account for those things and have them properly thought out. Failing to do so puts your company at risk, and that's just reckless, considering that the alternative is just for you to use a few secure apps. That's just it – there are no other requisites for you to consider.

As you can see for yourself, there is a tremendous amount of different things which an ethical hacker or an organization of the kind is going to handle in order to ensure that everything is handled perfectly. This is the main reason for which you need to ensure that you go ahead and take those into proper consideration if you are to circumvent those defenses and ensure that everything is handled perfectly. Unfortunately, this is far from being an easy task. There are a lot of things which you'd have to consider. Luckily for you, we've laid out quite a few of them down below. But, before that, let's take a look at another protection plan for the majority of the individual users. It's simple, and it's particularly quick and effective if you are on the other side of the computer.

# *Chapter 18: Hacking stuff – methods and approaches*

Now that you are very well aware of the things that you'd have to beware off if your victim decides to go professional, you should be capable of assessing the efforts which are needed to actually hack into someone's system. This is something that should be completely out of the question as the chances are that you will get in trouble. However, as we mentioned above, for the sake of being able to prevent attacks, it's important to know how they work.

Now that we are here, we would provide you with actionable knowledge on how to actually go through certain hacking undertakings. These are going to provide you with advanced and actionable information on how to actually hack some stuff. We've addressed a few very interesting methods – hacking administrator passwords as well as WhatsApp accounts. This should provide you with some technically advanced insight on how to handle these endeavors so let's go right ahead and take a look.

## How to Hack Administrator Passwords

Hacking an administrator password on Windows 10 is still possible in a convenient manner. Now, the first thing that you would need to know is that there are quite a lot of tools available online which are going to enable you to hack all sorts of accounts, including those who are usually found on mobile Android and iOS devices such as Skype, Facebook, Viber, WhatsApp and much more. However, when it comes to hacking a Windows 10 administrator account password, here is what you need to do, without purchasing any kind of external software.

This is a way for you to reset the passwords on any non-administrator accounts. However, in order to do so, you would need to have administrator privileges. The step-by-step instruction is as it follows.

1. The first thing you would need to do is to open the command prompt. You can do this by hitting Start, Run – type "cod" and hit Enter.

2. After that, you need to type "net user" and once again hit Enter.

3. The system is now going to provide you with a list of user accounts which could be found on the computer. Now, for the sake of the example, let's say that there is an account with the name Patrick. You have to do the following:

4. Type in "net user Patrick" and press the Enter button. Now, the system is going to require you to enter the new password for this particular account. You have already successfully managed to reset the password without Patrick knowing anything of the kind.

This is a fairly quick and easy way for you to hack every Windows 10 administrator password as long as you are granted some privileges. In any case, this is a fairly helpful trick to know as you can easily restrict access to the computer or you can get access to the system in order to remove different restrictions. For instance, a lot of parents are putting in parental control on the computer for their teenagers. However, if you are capable of accessing the administrator panel, you can easily overrun those restrictions without your parents even knowing about it. This could give you the access to unlimited gaming time that you've been craving.

In any case, this is a quick and helpful hacking tip that you could use in order to reset the password of a certain computer. Unless the original administrator finds out the password, he wouldn't have access to the panel at all.

**How to Hack a WhatsApp Account – Tips and Tricks**

WhatsApp is without a doubt one of the most commonly used messengers out there. With this in mind, learning how to hack an account might turn out to be quite helpful in certain situations. Of course, the easiest way for you would be to get specifically designated software which is going to "spy" on the user, thus capturing all of his personal information, including the account name and the password. However, this is usually going to cost you a certain amount of money that you may be reluctant to pay. Luckily, there are other ways to do so, even though they are a bit more challenging. Nevertheless, let's take a look at one of them.

## Mac Address Spoofing – The Hard Way

Apart from using specially designed software, you could also try this particular way to hack a WhatsApp Account. It involves spoofing the Mac address of a target smartphone through your own phone. However, this is more complicated, and it's likely to take you sometime to implement it. It's not particularly hard, per say, but it's definitely harder. It's also going to require some fairly technical skills. Below, you are going to find all the tips and the tricks that you can use to do so.

1. Find the Mac address of the target phone whose account you'd like to hack. In order to do so, you have to determine whether it's an Android or an iOS phone. If it's an Android go to settings, about device, status and click on the Wi-Fi MAC Address. If it's an iOS go to Settings, general, about and click on Wi-Fi Address. This is the first step you need to take.

2. Once you have obtained the address of the phone you like to hack, you need to spoof it.

3. Upon doing so, you are going to obtain the Mac address of the target phone and all you got to do install WhatsApp on your own and use the target phone number. You are now going to be in possession of an exact replica, and all of the messages, both outgoing and incoming are going to be received by you.

Even though this could be a quite challenging endeavor, it's a relatively uncomplicated way to hack someone's account without him even knowing it. The only thing you'd have to take into account is the access to his Mac address which could be the actual tricky part of the activity.

## ICloud Hacks - The things to consider

Why do you need an email account for iCloud?

In order to access the possibilities that iCloud provides, you would have to set up and email account and register it. This is going to be your personal ID, and every time you want to access the database, you would have to enter it along with your password.

## Benefits of using iCloud

Once you have registered your iCloud email account, you can start enjoying the benefits of the application. Basically, you will be presented with additional space to store different type of information. You can use it to back up important files, photos or any kind of data you find relevant. By doing this, you ensure that if something happens to your device, you would be able to restore the data which is being stored on your personal iCloud account. This way you won't have to worry about losing your device.

## Retrieve forgotten ID

It's not uncommon for people to forget the exact details of the iCloud email account. You can forget the username or the password, but in both cases, you won't be able to access the data on the iCloud. The procedure is rather simple. You have to reach the login screen and hit the link for forgotten IDs. You will be asked to enter an email address or an alternative one if you have forgotten your main account. This is so the staff can send you a new password on the email and so that you can once again access the information on the application.

## Hacks for iCloud – what do they do

Typically iOS and Mac devices pride themselves as being incredibly hard to get hacked. For the most part, this is true. However, the advancement of source codes has made it possible and currently there are different hacks that could easily get through your iCloud securities.

## How does it work?

An iCloud hack could be designated for a variety of reasons. Typically the most common one of them would be to get your account username and password so it can be accessed by a third party. The most usual fraud to which people fall involves opening unwanted email letters. They often consist of some sort of hacking software. Once you open the letter, the sender of the email gains access to your personal information and could easily access your iCloud.

## How to protect yourself

Normally, experts advise using anti-hacking software such as an anti-virus program. This piece of software is designated to detect malicious interference and disable it before it could reach any valuable information. However, not every iCloud hack is going to be detectable, and you might be exposed even if you are using an anti-virus. This is why the protection lies within your hands. The best thing you can do is to avoid opening suspicious emails from unknown senders. They normally follow a certain pattern which you can easily pick up. Another thing you can do is to avoid opening dangerous links that your anti-virus software warns you about. That's called preventive security.

# *Chapter 19: A few quick considerations: changing IP – would it help? (Infrastructure monitoring)*

This particular topic is widely discussed. While the prevailing opinion remains skeptical, it's also worth noting that there are certain ways in which you might remain entirely private on the Internet. For instance, if you change your IP you can mask your digital footprint. This won't allow crawlers to detect your information and to target you as a prospective lead. Hence, you can say goodbye to geo-targeted and content targeted ads. However, how to do so? Changing your IP isn't complicated.

**How to Change an IP Address**

Regardless of whether you are using a Windows 10, a Mac or a Linux OS, the truth is that changing your IP could be very handy in certain situations. If you are experiencing difficulties logging into certain websites with your Chrome Browser or through your Android or iOS phone, this might be due to the fact that your IP isn't accepted. What is more, you might want to hide your IP or change it directly after a certain operation for your own personal reasons. Let's take a look at how this is done exactly.

Every single time you connect to the Internet your Internet Service Provider is going to assign an IP address to your personal computer which is making it possible for the websites and the applications to properly keep track of all of your online activities as well as to pinpoint your actual physical location. In order to prevent your entire Internet privacy, you might have to change your IP address.

## Using a VPN Service

The best way to change your IP address, using a VPN proxy is without a doubt the fastest and most secure way to do so. There are quite a lot of VPN service providers out there; some are free, some are not – it's your call. However, you have to understand that this brings a certain set of advantages. You can bypass regional blocks in order to get access to sites and other content which is otherwise restricted to your particular location.

## Change Your IP by Restarting your Router

Now, in order for this to be effective, you have to know whether your ISP gets dynamic IP or not. If he does, all you need to do is turn off your router for a few seconds to up to a minute and then turn it back on. You are going to be assigned to a different IP, which is pretty convenient.

Keep in mind that this is also quite convenient when it comes to online gaming. There are plenty of games which are restricted in certain locations and the only way to actually bypass this restriction is through a different IP. What is more, you will be able to rest assured that your IP is virtually untraceable unless it's put through thorough investigation and even in this case it might not be uncovered. In any case, using a different IP or changing your current one is definitely quite handy in certain situations and knowing how to do so could be of help.

Of course, there are other considerations that you need to account for. This is especially true if you are an enterprise. Sure, changing your IP every now and then can help you out slightly, but that's not an effective solution. There are a few different things that you might want to account for, including the following.

## 1. End Point Security

With End Point Security being one of the fundamental concepts of an efficient organization's structure, companies can be ready to guide you in its preparation and deployment. Experts have solid knowledge of the bleeding edge solutions that can fortify your infrastructure.

## 2. Network Security

When it comes to security, there should be no shortcomings, yet a lot of companies seem to have dedicated the insufficient amount of attention to their Network Security. Allow a company to independently evaluate your network and provide you with the most up-to-date industry-accepted implementation solutions that can mitigate the risk at a very cost-effective scale without compromising neither quality nor effort. Gap analysis can provide you with the means to address and optimize your capabilities, and you can rely on expertise to guide you on the best suitable method, designed to fit your specific needs.

## 3. Infrastructure Monitoring

With the rapid growth of IT Infrastructure, companies can no longer rely on the manual and error-prone method of human monitoring. Companies can provide you with the means and expertise to benefit immensely from scalable monitoring systems, tailored to meet your custom requirements. Experts can delve into the depths of your IT Infrastructure and analyze your business processes and critical IT Infrastructure, thus introducing the necessary means to reduce the risk of malicious or unforeseen events impacting your business. Solutions can target a variety of vectors starting from end users to your applications, servers, devices or online presence. The alarms and indicators that engineers can provide you with will allow you to address all impactful events in the promptest of manners.

It's safe to say that these are the very first layer of basic protection that you can go through. Of course, it's also critical to understand that you need to undertake the necessary actions to prevent the threat.

Now, let's proceed with the good stuff. Let's take a look at a few ways to actually hack something.

# *Chapter 20: Advance hacking tips – the things to consider*

Now, as you are already introduced to the basics of hacking and you are well aware of the things that you would have to circumvent in case of an ethical hacking security check, it's only logical to keep going with a few advanced hacking tips and tricks. Of course, there isn't a lot of publicly available information on the internet and the reason is quite logical – hacking is illegal so websites who offer assistance in this particular sphere are rather sought after.

However, being the professionals that we are, we'd like to provide you with a few particularly helpful techniques and tips that might help you get ahead. Of course, you should understand that hacking is, indeed, illegal and you will be committing these at your own risk and free will.

## 1. Hacking a BSNL Broadband for enhanced speed

Now, if you are a BSNL broadband user, there is a high chance that you are facing common and rather regular DNS issues. The truth is that their DNS servers are just not responsive enough. The look up is going to take a significant amount of time and in the majority of cases it would just time out. What's the solution? Well, there is a small and rather interesting hack for it. You should use a simple third party DNS server instead of your BSNL DNS. Or, of course, you could always run your own one such as DJBDNS. The truth is that the easiest way for you to go is to use OpenDNS. However, you would have to reconfigure your own network to use the DNS servers as it follows:

- 208.67.222.222 and
- 208.67.220.220

Of course, you can find additional and particularly comprehensive information and instructions which are specific to your OS and your BSNL modem on the website of Open DNS. The truth is that once we reconfigured this, all the DNS issues where gone. This might not be a hack, per say, but it's a convenient way of getting rid of a problem which is actually disturbing.

### 2. Hacking a password with a USB Pen Drive

Now, this is another thing that you might be capable of doing. You can hack passwords using a simple USB Pen Drive. This is mainly due to the fact that Windows OS is storing almost all passwords which are used regularly and on a daily basis, including the ones for certain instant messengers. What is more, Windows OS is also going to store other passwords such as for your FTP accounts, Outlook Express, POP, SMTP and others as well as auto-complete passwords for a range of different browsers.

Using certain password recovery tools and a Pen Drive, you are capable of creating your own root kit and, therefore, hack passwords from the computer of another person. To do this, you will need the following:

**1. MessenPass** – this is an application which recovers passwords for the majority of the instant messengers.

**2. Mail PassView** – this is another tool which will recover different passwords for various email programs. This one can also recover web-based email accounts such as Gmail, for instance, but you have to use the associated programs.

**3. IE Passview** – this is a very small utility which will help your reveal different passwords which are stored by IE.

There are other tools which are specific for the programs that you want to recover password for. With this in mind, using the following technique and combining it with the proper tool, you can get the password that you want. Now, below is a hacking technique in a step by step manner which is going to help you cut tremendously.

**1.** Download all of the tools mentioned above (alongside additional ones that you want), extract all of them and copy the executable files (.exe) on your Pen drive.

**2.** Create a Notepad document and write the following right there into it:

[autorun]

open=launch.bat

ACTION= Perform a Virus Scan

Once you are done, go ahead, save the file and rename it to autorun.inf. This is also the file that you need to copy directly on your Pen drive as well.

**3.** Create another Notepad document and go ahead to right the following sequence:

| Start | mspass.exe | /stext | mspass.txt |
|-------|------------|--------|------------|
| start | mailpv.exe | /stext | mailpv.txt |
| start | iepv.exe | /stext | iepv.txt |
| start | pspv.exe | /stext | pspv.txt |

start passwordfox.exe /stext passwordfox.txt

This is the file that you need to save and rename to launch.bat. Once you are done, go ahead and place it on your pen drive. Now that you are through with this, your root kit is basically ready and you can start hacking passwords. Just follow the steps below:

**1.** Insert the pen drive on your friend's computer and the auto run window is going to pop instantly.

**2.** Select the first option in the box – it should be to perform a virus scan.

**3.** All of the tools which were uploaded on your pen drive will be stored within the .txt file.

Now, you are all packed with precious passwords. Also, keep in mind that this is going to work on Windows 2000, XP as well as on Windows Vista. However, it won't work on other operating systems. You should also account for the fact that this is a comprehensive method and you can create the root kit in a matter of minutes as long as you get the tools downloaded and unzipped. There is nothing so complicated and, as you can see, there is absolutely no need for different coding skills and you can handle this quickly and conveniently without any additional effort. You will be able to collect passwords without your friends or colleagues noticing it.

Of course, there are quite a lot of different hacking tips and tricks, we've also covered some administration hacking tips and WhatsApp account hacking – check them up down below. These are convenient and definitely tremendously helpful. You should be careful, though, because you could potentially get caught doing it. Make sure that you exercise caution – it's best to do it to someone who's not aware. (How To Hack Passwords Using a USB Drive)

# *Chapter 21: Why is Linux the best OS for hackers?*

Now, one of the most common questions that the majority of people tend to ask is related to the operating system. If you are advanced in the fields of hacking, you should already be aware of the fact that the best system for hacking is Linux. The reason for this is quite comprehensive. As a matter of fact, there are at least 15 reasons that we are going to take a look at right now.

The truth is that Linux is an open source OS which means that you could easily tweak different things up. Regardless of this, there are quite a lot of different things for which you should definitely consider using the OS for your hacking undertakings.

So, without any further ado, let's go right ahead and take a look at some of them.

### 1. Open Source

With the world of software development being as rapid and dynamic as it is today, you need to understand that hacking requires a lot of knowledge and the ability to actually modify operating system codes. This is where Linux is so handy and appropriate – you will be capable of doing so with the biggest ease in comparison to other operating systems, which is definitely something that you want to take into account. What is more, the majority of tools that you will be using are also open source, and therefore you could modify them as well.

### 2. Compatibility

Now, this is another critical consideration that you have to account for. Linux OS is fully compatible with all of the actual UNIX software packages. What is more, it is also capable of supporting all of the common file formats which are there, hence giving a significant advantage in comparison to other OS like Windows, for example.

### 3. Quick, fast and easy install process

The majority of the distributions of Linux are going to come with particularly easy and user-friendly setup programs and installations. What is more, it's also known that a lot of those tools are particularly easy to use. You should also be aware that the overall boot time of the OS is far quicker than other operating systems, which is one of the greatest benefits for the majority of the hackers.

### 4. Stability

That's just it. Linux won't require you to reboot it periodically like Windows in order to maintain high performance levels. In fact, Linux won't freeze up, and it won't slow down over time because of certain memory leaks as well as other things of this type. You can easily use the OS for years without any significant issues.

### 5. Network Friendliness

As you certainly know, one of the most important things for every hacker is connectivity. A lot of the hacking endeavors such as DDoS would require flawless network connectivity, and this is where Linux actually shines. The fact that the operating system is an open source solution means that it manages to network over it and it also provides a range of different commands which are capable of being used to test different network penetrations. As you must most certainly know from what we've written above when it comes to penetration testing, this is one of the most important properties to consider. What is more, you also need to understand that Linux OS is much more reliable and it is going to make your network back up a lot faster than any other operating system is currently available. This is particularly important when it comes to it.

### 6. Multitasking

Hacking is a complex process which requires the careful execution of a few tasks at a time. Linux is specifically designed to allow the user to compile and handle a few things at the same time. For instance, you could be caring out a coding hack while at the same time running certain botnet applications. This is definitely one of the reasons for which almost every hacker out there would actually use it.

### 7. Full use of your hard disk

Being a hacker is a lot like being a collector of personal information. This is particularly true if you will be targeting groups of people or organizations with a significant number of people working in them. Linux allows the full usage of the hard disk, which is going to provide you with a lot more leeway and a higher margin for storage in comparison to Windows OS.

### 8. Flexibility

That's just it – Linux is particularly flexible. It could be used in order to run high-performance server apps, desktop apps as well as embedded systems as well. This is a particularly critical predisposition towards adequate hacking, and as such, it needs to be accounted for as a significant pro.

### 9. Low Cost

This is an important consideration when it comes to it. You should understand that expenses are going to pile up if you are going to be conducting hacking efforts. However, one thing that you can save off money from is your OS. Linux is an open source, as you must surely know already and as such it's freely available for the users on the internet. What is more, you should also know that the applications which run on it are also free of any significant cost. This is definitely an important consideration.

## 10. a lot less vulnerable

Essentially, this is one of the biggest advantages of Linux over other operating systems. Even though accessibility to different systems is absolutely granted nowadays, Linux remains the most reliable one. It has a lot of vulnerability if not used properly but if you know what you are doing, there is no secure option than this one.

Now, of course, it's also worth noting that there is a lot more to Linux OS than just those 10 points on top of it. It provides support for the majority of the programming languages. At the same time, the majority of the tools that you will be using for hacking are written for it. Some of the most popular examples in this particular regard include Metasploit as well as Nmap. They are ported to windows, but the majority of the capabilities can be transferred from Linux, which is the main designation. Unlike Windows, Linux also takes your privacy particularly serious, and that's definitely something that you want to account for. One of the most significant advantages is that you wouldn't need any type of drivers in order to actually use the OS functionally and effectively. This is definitely a huge benefit. And, there are a lot more to these than you might actually think.

Now that we've gone through all of the perks that hackers do like about Linux, it's also important to note that this isn't the only available solution if you want to start off your hacking undertakings. There are quite a lot of different operating systems which are going to be at least as successful. The important thing that you need to take into account is that you need to ensure that you are using the OS which is convenient for what you have in mind. This is absolutely critical. With this in mind, we've decided to take a look at a few other OS which are available to the user and which are particularly great for hacking. So, without any further ado, let's take a quick look.

## 1. Backtrack

This is another well-known operating system based on Linux much like Kali Linux. It is best known for being used throughout the previous years as the operating system designated for cracking networks and penetration testing. What is more, it's amongst the only OS on the market which is capable of performing different hacks with significant privacy. There are quite a lot of features that you might want to account for, including:

- **Cisco OCS Mass Scanner** – this is a very reliable and particularly quick scanner which allows Cisco routers to actually test default telnet as well as password enabling.
- It offers a tremendous amount of collected exploits and also conventional software like regular browsers, for instance.
- Wi-Fi drivers are actually supporting packet injection as well as monitor mode. There is also an available integration of Metasploit as well.

## 2. Pentoo

It goes without saying that Gentoo is without a doubt amongst the best operating systems for active hackers. In order to get it going, you just need to create a USB which is bootable and run it on your PC. After this, there are absolutely no requirements that you'd have to go and all that is left for you to do is to conduct different hacking attacks. There are quite a lot of comprehensive features, which are specifically designated to make your life as a hacker a lot easier, so let's go ahead and take a look.

- It's available in both 32 and 64-bit versions. The latter has a significant increase in the speed in comparison to the 32bit version.
- Includes the necessary environment in order to crack different passwords using CUDA, OpneCL, GPGPU as well as other configurations.

- It's built on hardened Linux which includes a particularly hardened toolchain as well as the kernel which has a lot of extra patches.

## 3. Nodezero

Now, this is another particularly good OS which is designated for hacking entirely. It is being developed after the necessity of quite a lot of different things which aren't actually present on different Linux-based operating systems.

## 4. Parrot Security Forensic

This is an OS which is actually based on Debian GNU and Linux, and it's mixed with Frozen Box and Kali Linux. The main designation is to create the most brilliant operating system which is going to provide you with tremendously beneficial security testing and penetration testing experience for security testers and for attackers as well. This is an OS which is specifically designated for IT security as well as penetration testing. It has quite a lot of different features which are brilliant for that, and they include:

- Custom as well as properly hardened Linux 4.3 kernel. It also comes with rolling release upgrade line which is particularly important.
- It has custom anti-forensic capabilities which are definitely something that you might be interested in.
- Apart from that, you can also enjoy custom interfaces for crypt setup as well as for CPG, which is definitely to be considered.
- It supports the most famous Digital Forensic tools as well as different frameworks which are convenient enough.

## 5. Arch Linux

This is a Linux distribution designated for computers which are based on the architectures of x86-64 and IA-32. It is composed mainly out of free as well as of open-source software, and it is known to support the significant involvement of the community, which is definitely something that you need to account for. Now, let's take a look at the feature which is going to make this a good choice.

- Arch Linux takes advantage of the Pacman, package manager. This is designed to couple with obviously simple binary packages, and they come with a comprehensive and easy to use the system.

- It comes with a rolling release system which is going to allow for a quick one-off installation process. The upgrades are going to be perpetual and automatic once this is completed.

- It strives to keep the packages which are additional close to the original as much as it's possible in order to ensure the proper and optimal performance of the system.

In any case, it's worth noting that there are quite a lot of additional options that you might be interested in when it comes to it. Some of the other interesting hacking operating systems include BackBox, the Network Security Toolkit, GnackTrack, and Bugtraq as well. Of course, Kali Linux remains the most overly preferred and reliable option that you can go for. The reasons are particularly numerous, and we've listed some of the major ones above so make sure to take them into account.

The OS is an integral and particularly important part of your hacking endeavors, and it's absolutely critical that you take it into proper consideration. With this in mind, choosing one of the above is without a doubt going to be a good choice that you might want to take into account.

# *Chapter 22: Raspberry Pi – An Overview*

The Raspberry Pi has many incredible features. The largest appeal of the Raspberry Pi computer is that it is a small size, and is also affordable. The Raspberry Pi can be used as a traditional computer by simply being plugged into a TV and a keyboard. Since 2012, there have been many models of the Raspberry Pi released to the public, each with their own improvements and changes.

Approximately the size of a credit card and available for as little as $5USD, the intended purpose of the Raspberry Pi was to bring affordable computer options to everyone. Below, we are going to take a brief look at the different models of Raspberry Pi.

**Raspberry Pi 1 Model A** – This was the original model of the Raspberry Pi. Released in February 2012. This was followed up late by the Raspberry Pi 1 Model A Plus which was released in November 2014, which featured a larger hard drive and a lower price point.

**Raspberry Pi 1 Model B**– The Generation 1 and 1 Plus of the Model B Raspberry Pi were released in April 2012 and July 2014 respectively. The 1 Plus had a lower price point than the original Model B and featured a microSD slot instead of the standard SD slot.

**Raspberry Pi Zero** – This was a smaller model that was released in November 2015. The size of the Zero was smaller and it had a reduced input and output. This is the cheapest model of Raspberry Pi that is currently available for purchase. The original Zero did not include video input. However, a second version released in May 2016 included video input options similar to other models.

**Raspberry Pi 2** – This model included more ram than any of the previous models and was released in February 2015. This model is at the high end of all Raspberry Pi products and can be found for just $35USD.

**Raspberry Pi 3 Model B** – This is the newest model of Raspberry Pi. Released in

February 2016, the Raspberry Pi 3, Model B is bundled with the additions including onboard Wi-Fi, Bluetooth, and USB boot capabilities. We will cover more on this later in this book.

There are a few things that are common among all the versions of Raspberry Pi. This includes the Broadcom system on a chip, which features a CPU (Central Processing System) that is compatible with ARM, as well as on-chip GPU (Graphics Processing Unit).

The boards all have between one and four USB slots, as well as an HDMI slot, composite video output and a 3.5 mm phone jack for audio capabilities.

The creators of Raspberry Pi provide *Raspbian*, which is a Debian-based Linux distribution for download. It also provides third party *Ubuntu*, *Windows 10* IOT Core, RISC OS, and other specialized media center distributions. While the Raspberry Pi supports many programming languages, it promotes Python and Scratch as its main programming language. You also have the option of open source or closed source firmware, although the default firmware is closed source.

# *Chapter 23: Raspberry Pi 3 – Software Specifications*

One of the neat things about the Raspberry Pi 3 – Model B is that you can run almost any software on it. While it primarily uses *Raspbian*, which is a Debian-based Linux operating system, you are not limited to using this. In this chapter, we are going to run through all the different operating systems, driver APIs, firmware and other third party application software that will be accessible to you for use on the Raspberry Pi 3 – Model B.

**Operating Systems**

On the official Raspberry Pi website, you will have access to Ubuntu Mate, Snappy Ubuntu Core, Windows 10 IoT Core, and RISC OS, as well as specialized distributions for the Kodi media center and classroom management. Below we are going to cover every operating system that can be used, categorized by those that are Linux based and those that not Linux based.

*Linux Based Operating Systems:*

<u>Alpine Linux</u> – This is a Linux distribution that is based on *musl* and *BusyBox*. It has been primarily designed for those power users who require more security, simplicity, and resource efficiency.

<u>Android Things</u> – This is an embedded version of the Android operating system that is designed for IoT device development.

<u>Ark OS</u> – This operating system has been designed for website and email self-hosting.

<u>CentOS</u> – This is a newer operating system that is only available for Raspberry Pi 2 and newer.

<u>Diet Pi</u> – This operating system includes a diverse range of servers that are ideal for media, Minecraft, VPN, and much more.

<u>Fedora 25</u> – This is another newer operating system that is only available for the newer Raspberry Pi models.

<u>Gentoo</u> – This operating system is ideal for users who want full control of the software that

they use on their Raspberry Pi 3.

Instant WebKiosk – This operating system is ideal for users who are looking for digital signage purposes such as web and media views.

Kali Linux – This operating system is a Debian derived distro that has been designed for digital forensics and penetration testing.

Kano OS – This operating system is one that you can build and customize to be exactly what you want it to be for you. Completely free, this is a great choice if you want to have full control over your operating system.

MinePeon – This operating system has been designed to be dedicated to mining cryptocurrency.

Moebius – This is another operating system that is based on Debian. This operating system is a light ARM HF distribution that uses Raspbian repository but fits onto a 128 MB SD card. This operating system only offers minimal services and has had its memory use optimized to keep it small.

NARD SDK – This is a software development kids that is intended for industrial embedded systems.

OpenSUSE – This is another operating system that gives you full control over creating the code for your system.

OpenWrt – This operating system is primarily used to route network traffic on embedded devices.

Pardus ARM – This operating system is another option for a Debian derived system. This is the light version of the Pardus operating system that is popular with the Turkish Government.

Pidora – This is a Fedora Remix that has been optimized for use on the Raspberry Pi.

ROKOS – This operating system is another Rasbian based option that is integrated for use with Bitcoin and OKCash cryptocurrencies.

Tingbot OS – This operating system has been designed to be used primarily with the Tingbot add-on as well as running Tide applications. This operating system is also based on the Raspbian operating system.

Tiny Core Linux – This operating system is designed to run primarily in RAM. It is a minimal Linux operating system where the primary focus is to provide a base system using

BusyBox and FLTK.

Void Linux – This operating system is a rolling release Linux distribution that has been designed and implemented from scratch. Void Linux provides images based on musl or glibc.

WTware for Raspberry Pi – This is a free operating system that is used for the creation of Windows thin client.

Xbian – This operating system uses the Kodi open source digital media center.


*Not Linux Based Operating Systems:*

Genode OS Framework – This operating system is a toolkit that is used to build highly secure special purpose operating systems. This is not the operating system that would be best for those who are just starting out, however, if you have a lot of experience with coding, this is a good choice.

HelenOS – This operating system is a portable multi-server that is microkernel-based.

NetBSD – This operating system is another that will allow you to create the coding and use your Raspberry Pi 3 – Model B however, you decide.

Plan 9 – This is an open source operating system that is similar to Unix. It was originally developed at Bell Labs as a research operating system. When you are using Plan 9, everything is treated as a file regardless of whether it is a local or network resource.

Xv6 – This is a modern version of the Sixth Edition Unix operating system that has been re-implemented for teaching purposes. It is easily ported to the Raspberry Pi from MIT xv6 which can be booted from NOOBS (New Out of Box Software).

Media Center Operating Systems – If you are looking for operating systems that are going to run your Raspberry Pi 3 – Model B as a media center your best options are OSMC, OpenELEC, LibreELEC, XBIAN, and Rasplex.

Audio Operating Systems – If you want to use your Raspberry Pi 3 – Model B for audio, the best operating systems are going to include Volumio, Pimusicbox, Runeaudio, and moOdeaudio.

Retrogaming Operating Systems – If you want to use your Raspberry Pi 3 – Model B to play retro games, the ideal operating systems include Retropie, Recalbox, Happi Game Centre, Lakka, ChameleonPi, and Piplay.

### Driver APIs

Raspberry Pi 3 – Model B has the capability to use a VideoCore IV GPU through a binary blob. The binary blob is loaded into the GPU when it is booted from the SD card. Much of the driver work was originally done using the closed source GPU code, although there are software applications such as OpenMAX, OpenGL ES, or OpenVG which can be used to call an open course driver in the VideoCore IV GPU driver code.

### Firmware

The official firmware of the Raspberry Pi 3 – Model B is a closed course binary blob that is freely redistributable. There is also open source firmware that is available minimally.

### Third Party Application Software

As well as the operating systems that we covered in this chapter, there are many options for other software that can be put onto your Raspberry Pi 3 – Model B from third parties. In this section, we are going to briefly look at some of the more popular third party applications.

Mathematica – Raspbian includes a full installation of this software for free. This allows programs to be run from either a command line interface or from a notebook interface. Some of the language functions allow for accessing connected devices.

Minecraft – In February 2013, a version of Minecraft was released for Raspberry Pi that allows you to modify the game world with code. This is the only official version of Minecraft that allows this.

RealVNC – RealVNC's remote access server and viewer software are included with the Raspbian operating system. This includes the new capture technology which allows content to be directly rendered as well as non-X11 applications to be viewed and controlled remotely.

UserGate Web Filter – In 2013, Entensys, a security vendor based in Florida, announced they would be porting Usergate Web Filter to the Raspberry Pi Platform.

## Software Development

In addition to the addition applications listed above, there are programs available that can help you learn more about developing software. Learning how to develop software will help you be able to use the Raspberry Pi 3 – Model B to its fullest potential.

<u>AlgoID</u> – This is a program that is ideal for teaching programming to children as well as beginners in the programming world.

<u>Julia</u> – This is a programming language that is both interactive and able to be used across multiple platforms. IDE's for Julia are also available including June and JuliaBerry, which is a Pi specific repository.

<u>Scratch</u> – This teaching tool uses visual blocks that stack to teach IDE. MIT's Life Long Kindergarten group originally developed this. The version that was created for Pi is heavily optimized for the limited computing resources that are available and work well with the Squeak Smalltalk system.

Now that you are aware of the software options that are available for you to use with your Raspberry Pi 3 – Model B, we are going to explore how you can go about configuring your Raspberry Pi to do what you want it to do.

# *Chapter 24: Raspberry Pi 3 – Model B Hardware Specifications*

There have been several evolutions in the hardware that the Raspberry Pi offers. In this chapter, we are going to focus on the Raspberry Pi 3 – Model B specifically.

For the purpose of keeping this book easy to read for those of you who aren't as familiar with the technological jargon, while keeping it interesting for those of you who don't need as in depth of an explanation, this chapter is going to be broken down into sections that allow you to skim through and find the information you are looking for without having to read every explanation.

## Wireless Radio – Broadcom BCM43438

This wireless radio has been expertly built directly into the board to keep the cost of the Raspberry Pi down. It is also so small; you are going to be able to see the markings through a microscope or magnifying glass. The Broadcom BCM43438 chip gives the Raspberry Pi 2.4 GHZ 802.11n wireless LAN, Bluetooth Low Energy, and Bluetooth 4.1 Classic radio support. This is what is going to allow you to connect your Raspberry Pi to the internet, both through a wired connection as well as through a wireless connection.

## SoC – Broadcom BCM2837

This SoC (System on Chip) has been built specifically for the Raspberry Pi 3 – Model B. This SoC features four high-performance ARM Cortex-A53 processing cores which run at 1.2GHz and have 32kB level one and 512kB level two memory. It also has a Video Core IV graphics processor and is also linked to the one gigabyte LPDDR2 memory module that is located on the rear of the board.

## GPIO – 40-Pin Header, Populated

The GPIO (General Purpose Input Output) header is the same on this Raspberry Pi as it has been going back through most of the Raspberry Pi models. This means that any existing GPIO hardware is going to work with the Raspberry Pi 3 – Model B without any further modifications needed. The only change that has been made to this part of the Raspberry Pi is a change to which UART is exposed on the pins. However, this doesn't affect usage as the operating system internally handles it.

### USB Chip – SMSC LAN9514

This is another part of the Raspberry Pi that hasn't changed from the Raspberry Pi 2. The SMSC LAN9514 adds 10/100 Ethernet connectivity as well as four USB channels to the board. The chip connects to the SoC through a single USB channel, acting as a USB to Ethernet adaptor as well as a USB hub.

To sum up all the information above:

**SoC**: Broadcom BCM2837

**CPU**: 4× ARM Cortex-A53, 1.2GHz

**GPU**: Broadcom VideoCore IV

**RAM**: 1GB LPDDR2 (900 MHz)

**Networking**: 10/100 Ethernet, 2.4GHz 802.11n wireless

**Bluetooth**: Bluetooth 4.1 Classic, Bluetooth Low Energy

**Storage**: microSD

**GPIO**: 40-pin header, populated

**Ports**: HDMI, 3.5mm analog audio-video jack, 4× USB 2.0, Ethernet, Camera Serial Interface (CSI), Display Serial Interface (DSI)

Now that we are all familiar with the hardware that is inside the Raspberry Pi 3 – Model B, we are going to have a look at the software.

# *Chapter 25: Configuring Raspberry Pi*

Once you have your Raspberry Pi 3 – Model B in your possession, you are going to want to get it set up and ready to use. The good news is that setting it up is easy and takes less than thirty minutes. That means that before you know it, you are going to be ready to start doing some awesome stuff with your new piece of technology!

**Before You Start**

Before you get started, there are a few supplies you are going to need on hand in addition to the Raspberry Pi to get through the set-up process and move on to amazing projects.

<u>HDMI television or monitor</u> – You are going to need to connect your Raspberry Pi to a display which means that you need some sort of HDMI enabled screen. You don't need to use a full-sized monitor for your Raspberry Pi, and there are compact options on the market. There are also ways around using a monitor at all, which we will discuss later in this chapter.

<u>USB keyboard and mouse</u> – In order to be able to control your Raspberry Pi 3 – Model B, you are going to need to have a keyboard and mouse. Any USB keyboard and mouse will work for this.

<u>8GB MicroSD card and card reader</u> – Instead of using a hard drive, Raspberry Pi's operating system is installed with a MicroSD card. You are going to want at least 8Gb for this. Your computer might have a card reader. If it does not, all you are going to need is a cheap one,. Card readers can often be found for under $10 USD.

<u>Power Supply</u> – The Raspberry Pi 3 – Model B is powered by a micro USB, similar to the one you likely use for your cell phone. Since the Pi 3 – Model B has four USB ports, the best power supply is one that can provide at least 2.5A of power.

**Step One – Install Raspbian Onto Your MicroSD Card with NOOBs**

The first thing you are going to have to do before you can use your new Raspberry Pi 3 – Model B is to put Raspbian onto your MicroSD card. To do this, you first need to download the operating system on another computer and transfer it to your SD card. There are two ways you can do this. First, you can install Raspian manually. This required you to either know the command line, or external software. The second option, which is much simpler requires that you download and install NOOBs Since this is the easier option, this is the option we are going to review in this chapter.

1 – Put your SD card into your computer or SD card reader.

2 – Download NOOBs. Choose the option of "offline and network install." This option will include Raspbian in the download itself.

3 – You may need to format your SD card as FAT. If so, download the SD Association's Formatting Tool which can be found at sdcard.org. Simply set the "Format Size Adjustment" to "on" in the options menu, and your SD card will be formatted.

4 – Extract the Zip file. Once the extraction is complete, copy the entire folder contents to your SD card. Once the copy is complete, you can eject your SD card and insert it into your Raspberry Pi 3 – Model B.

**Step Two – Hook Up Your Raspberry Pi**

The next step is to connect your devices to your Raspberry Pi 3 – Model B. Doing this is very easy, since all you need to do is plug stuff into the USB ports. However, it is important to do this is in the order listed below to ensure that all of your devices are recognized when you boot your Raspberry Pi up.

1 – Connect your monitor to your Raspberry Pi

2 – Connect your USB mouse and keyboard

3 – If you are using an Ethernet cable for your router, connect it now.

4 – Connect your power adapter. Since your Raspberry Pi 3 – Model B doesn't have a power switch, as soon as you connect the power source it is going to turn on.

**Step Three – Set Up Raspbian**

When you first boot up NOOBs, it is going to be busy for a couple of minutes formatting the SD card and setting things up. Let it do what it needs to do. Eventually, there will be a screen that will come up asking you to install an operating system.

1 – At the bottom of the screen there is going to be a place where you can select your language and keyboard layout for your region.

2 – Check the box that is next to the Raspbian option and click install.

NOOBs will then run the installation process, which can take anywhere from ten to twenty minutes. Once it is complete, the Raspberry Pi will restart itself and then send you straight to the Raspbian desktop where you will have the ability to configure everything else.

**Step Four – Configure Your Raspberry Pi 3 – Model B**

Your Raspberry Pi is now mostly ready to go. In Raspbian you are going to see a start menu. In this start menu, you are going to be able to select applications, open a file browser, and execute other commands that you might expect to be able to do with an operating system. The first thing you should do is set up your Wi-Fi, as well as any Bluetooth devices you want to use, with your Raspberry Pi.

Connect to Your Wi-Fi Network

Connecting to Wi-Fi through your Raspbian is just as easy as any modern operating system you may be accustomed to working with.

1 – Click the network icon. It is located at the top right corner and looks like two computers.

2 – Select your Wi-Fi network name and enter your password.

That's it. You are now connected to your Wi-Fi network. You are only going to need to do this once, and it will work in both the command line and the graphical interface.

Connect Bluetooth Devices

If you want to use a Bluetooth enabled mouse or keyboard with your Raspberry Pi 3 – Model B, you are going to need to pair them. Depending on the device you are pairing, this process can vary a bit, but using the directions below, you shouldn't have any issues.

1 – Click on the Bluetooth icon that is in the upper right corner of your screen.

2 – Click the "Add Device" option

3 – Find the device that you want to pair your Raspberry Pi with and follow the directions that appear on the screen to pair them up.

Once you have followed the directions above, your Raspberry Pi 3 – Model B is ready for you to start playing around with. If something goes wrong and you end up somehow messing up the programming, you can also follow the above steps to reinstall Raspbian and start over.

**Connect to Your Raspberry Pi Remotely**

Occasionally you might find yourself in a position where you may want to access your Raspberry Pi remotely. Maybe you don't have access to a monitor, or you only have a laptop in the house. Whatever reason you may have for wanting to connect remotely, it's handy to know that there are options.

Connect to The Command Line Through SSH – You can use SSH from any computer to connect to the command line interface of your Raspberry Pi. While this option won't allow you to access a graphic interface, you can run any type of command from the Terminal application, and it'll execute on the Raspberry Pi. This is especially useful if you are working on a project that doesn't require a screen.

Use VNC To Use Your Home Computer as A Remote Screen – If your project requires that you do have a graphical interface, VNC (virtual network computing) to obtain it. You will be able to see the Raspberry Pi's desktop in a window on your computer desktop, and you will be able to control it like you are using the Pi. This isn't the best option for the day to day use as it is slow, but in the event that you only need to get a few things established and don't want to necessarily have to use the keyboard and mouse, this is an easy way to do so.

Now that you know how to get your Raspberry Pi 3 – Model B up and running, in the next chapter, we are going to look at some of the programming associated with your Raspberry Pi.

# *Chapter 26: Programming In Raspberry Pi*

The original purpose of the Raspberry Pi was to be able to teach people about technology. In this chapter, we are going to learn some of the basics of the two programming languages that are included in Raspbian, which is the recommended distribution for the Pi.

**Scratch**

This is a great language for those who are learning the basics of programming. Scratch doesn't require you to get the text perfect. Instead, everything is done by dragging and dropping program blocks into your script. This also means that you aren't going to have to remember any of the commands. For this example, we are going create a simple drawing program that will allow us to use the arrow keys to trace lines on the screen.

The first thing you are going to have to do is open Scratch. You will find Scratch in the **Menu**, under **Programming**. Once you have opened Scratch, you will see a screen with blocks of code, a scripts area, a stage where you can see your project, as well as some toolbars.

Now that we have the program open, we are going to create the code that will let us move the cat sprite around the screen.

We are going to use three separate blocks, each of which will be executed when a key is pressed. First, press the yellow control button, which is located on the left side of the screen near the top. Drag and drop the option "**When Space Key Pressed**" into the scripts box. This is going to create a script that will run whenever the space key is pressed. Use the drop-down menu and change **Space** to **Right Arrow**. Click on the blue motion button that is located next to the yellow control button and drag **Move 8 Steps** under **Right Arrow** in the scripts window. This will allow you to move the cat forward by pressing the right arrow.

Now that you have done that, create similar scripts that turn clockwise when the down key is pressed, and counter clockwise when the up key is pressed. Once you have finished that, we will be able to move around. However, we will need to add a block that will allow us to draw. Since we don't want to draw all the time, we will use Scratch's **pen up** and **pen**

**down** actions. When the pen is down, the cat will leave a line behind it. When the pen is up, the cat won't.

In order to toggle between having the pen up and the pen down, we are going to require the code to remember which state the pen is in. Programs use variables to do this. A variable is a chunk of memory that allows you to place data in and read data from. Before you are going to be able to use a variable, you are going to have to tell the computer to assign memory to it. We are also going to assign it a name that we can use to refer to it in the commands.

Go to **Variables**, in the same area you found control and motion, click on **Make a Variable,** and give it the name **Pen**. Once you have done this, you are going to see a selection of commands that are able to alter or use the variable. Now that we have a way to store the date, we are going to tell the computer to change its behavior based on what the variable is. This is done using an **If... Else** block. This is going to ask if a statement is true. If it is, it will execute the first block of code. If not, it will execute the second.

In our program, we are going to take the variable, **Pen**. If it is 0, we are going to put the pen down, then set it to one. Otherwise, we will lift the pen and set it to be 0. In this way, we are going to be able to toggle between the two states by using the spacebar.

Now you can move the cat around and draw a picture. However, wouldn't it be even better if you could insert a predefined item? We are going to learn how to add circles next. Technically it is going to be a twenty-four-sided shape, but it will look similar to a circle.

The method to do this is to **move forward 10**, then **rotate 15 degrees**, then **move forward 10**, then **rotate 15 degrees**, and keep doing this until you have completed the circle, which would require you to put in the same two lines twenty-four times. This would work, but it isn't the best way. Not only would it look terrible in the coding and be time consuming, but if you wanted to change the size of the circle, you would need to do this twenty-four times. The good news is, there is a better option.

Instead of writing out the code twenty-four times, can instead use a loop. A loop is a block that repeats itself. There are different types of loops, some that will keep going until a statement becomes false, and some that execute a set number of times. For this, we are going to use one that executes a set number of times.

You can find the loop option in the yellow control tab. We are going to use just two commands: **move forward 10**, and **rotate 15 degrees.** We will then set this to happen twenty-four times.

Now that you know how to use Scratch, you can play around with Scratch and discover just how much you can do with this programming software. (Peers, 2015)

## Python

While Scratch is great to help you to learn the basics of programming, sooner or later you are going to reach its limitations and want to move onto something new. Python is a popular general-purpose programming language that is also easy to learn.

The first thing you need to be aware of is that Python is entirely text-based. This doesn't mean that it is unable to create graphics, but rather that your program code is going to written text instead of the drag and drop blocks we used in Scratch.

Before you get started with Python, it is important to know that since Python is text-based, you can use any text editor to create your programs. Leafpad comes with Pi and is a great starting point. Avoid using word processors such as LibreOffice Writer as they mess up the formatting and won't allow your program to function correctly.

First, open the Pi **menu** and choose **Programming** and then **Python 3**. This is the command line, but since we want to access IDLE's text editor, we are going to choose **File** and **New** to create a new blank document. On the first line type:

**#!/usr/bin/python**

This line is going to tell the system to use the program python, in the folder /usr/bin/ to run the file. This is important to add to the start of all the programs you create with Python.

In the programming world, there is a long-standing tradition of having your first program output "Hello World!" and we aren't going to break it here! Leave the second line blank and on the third line type:

**Print "Hello World!"**

Save your work in a file called hello.py.

Skipping a line in your coding is not strictly necessary. However, it makes your code easier to read.

To run the program we just created, open a terminal and navigate to where you saved the file. The default will be your home folder. First, type the following command to tell the system the file is executable:

**$ chmod a+x hello.py**

Next, type this command to run your program:

**$ ./hello.py**

You should see Hello World! appear on the screen. This shows us that the system is running properly. However, this program is not a very useful program.

(Peers, 2015)

Like we did with Scratch, we are going to add some user input. With the Python program, we are going to need to add a variable to store what the user types are. Delete the line with Hello World, leaving the top line, and add the line:

**Name = raw_input('what is your name')**

This line is going to create the variable name, display the prompt, "what is your name?", and store what the user types are. We must place this in inverted commas so the computer can recognize it as a single chunk of text. We are then going to be able to use this variable to make our print statement a little more personal with the line:

**print 'Hello', name**

Since the computer is going to run the commands in order, this one needs to be below the previous one. If you were to reverse the order they are in, the computer will register an error because we are trying to use a variable before we have even created it. You can now save the file and enter **./hello.py** at the command line to run the program.

This makes the program more functional, but leaves it relatively lifeless. In order to make it more useful, we need to add a step where the computer must look at what was inputted and perform a different task based on that input. If you recall the **If** block in Scratch, we are going to do something similar here except, we are actually going to write the code. The basic structure is going to be:

**if :**

**code block**

This must be replaced with something that can be true or false. In our case, we are going to check if the name entered is a particular value:

**If name == 'Jane' :**

Why ==? Computers don't deal well with ambiguity. Every symbol or word that we use can only have one meaning. Otherwise, things start to get confusing. The equal sign, "=", is used to assign a value to a variable, so we need to use something else to check the equality. Again, we are going to enclose **Jane** in inverted commas so the computer can recognize it's text. The colon tells the computer that we have finished our expression, and we are about to tell it what to do.

We may want this **If** command to run through more than one line of code. This means that we need a way to group code into blocks. This is done using indents in Python. Indents can be either a space or a tab. However, it is crucial to use the same method throughout your project to avoid confusion. Python doesn't read the amount of indentation, but rather the number of indents you have made. Personally, I use two spaces for each indent, because that's how I was taught, and it makes it simple to keep it all the same.

Back to our programming. Now we want the computer to do something **if name == 'Jane'** so we have to tell the computer what we want it to do.

**if name == 'Jane' :**

  **print "Jane, you're awesome"**

Note that there are two spaces at the start of the second line. There are also double speech marks. This is because the text we have enclosed has an apostrophe in it. Since we don't want to be rude to all the people who aren't Jane, we are going to add an else block that runs whenever the above expression is false:

**else :**

  **print 'hello', name**

One last feature we are going to include is a loop. This is going to work similar to the one we created in Scratch, except it isn't going to only run twenty-four times. Instead, it will run until we tell it to stop. We are going to do this using a while look and the syntax:

**while :**

**code block**

We can have the program stop by entering the **name quit**. This means our **while** loop will be:

**while name !: 'quit' :**

For some reason, exclamation marks are often used to mean "not in the programming world". However, we are still left with a bit of a problem. If we put it before **name = raw_input...** we are going to produce an error because the computer doesn't know what **name** is. But if we put it after, it will only ask us to enter a name once, then spit the greeting out indefinitely, which is also not ideal.

There is a way to solve this. We are simply going to string the name before **while**. This stops the error and will always trigger the **while** expression. So, the program should look like this:

**#!/usr/bin/python**

**name = "**

**while name != 'quit' :**
**name = raw_input('What is your name?')**

**if name == 'Jane' :**
    **print "Jane, you're awesome"**
**else :**
    **print 'Hello', name**

You should note that there are four spaces before each print line. This is because they have been indented twice. Once for the **while** loop and once for the **if** statement. Now you can save this as hello.py and as before, run it with ./hello.py.

Both Scratch and Python are great programs to get started with, so now you can pick the one that appealed to you the most. In the next chapter, we are going to look at some sample project ideas that you can use to get started with programming your Raspberry Pi 3 –

Model B.

# *Chapter 27: Accessories For Your Raspberry Pi 3 – Model B*

Costing only $35, the Raspberry Pi is a great price, and it also very basic. However, there are many accessories you can get for your Raspberry Pi if you want to spend the money. In this chapter, we are going to briefly look at some of the available accessories and the pros and cons of each one. We are also going to take a look at what you would get from each accessory, whether that be aesthetic, functionality or something else.

**Raspberry Pi 3 Starter/Media Center Kit** – For anyone who is buying the Pi 3, particularly if it is the first Pi owned, a starter kit can be a huge benefit. It comes with a power supply, a case, an 8GB micro SD card, HDMI and Ethernet cables. It also includes NOOBs, Raspbian, and Kodi pre-installed.

**HDMI to VGA Adapter** – HDMI is very common. However, it's still not everywhere. If you have a monitor that is not HDMI enabled, or you just prefer VGA, this is one attachment that will make your life a lot easier.

**Raspberry Pi Heatsink** – The Raspberry Pi 3 – Model B produces heat. If you are going to be doing advanced projects, it is going to produce more heat. To extend the life of the processor, a heatsink is a great option.

**Raspberry Pi Touchscreen** – Touchscreens are everywhere, and if you are planning on making a Pi Phone or tablet, this is a great product to have. While most of the touchscreens you are going to find are only 480p, it is still better than a non-touch display.

**Camera Module** – Almost every device available these days has a camera. Adding a camera to your Raspberry Pi will allow you to use it as a video calling box, home security system or even as an actual camera.

**Pi Sense Hat** – There are some things you probably never considered you might need. Like temperature sensors, humidity sensors and an LED sensor. The PiSense Hat also has an accelerometer, a magnetic sensor, a five-button joystick, and a barometer. This makes it an essential tool for many projects.

**Adafruit RGB Matrix** – If you are hoping to make a stunning light show, or just need a basic display to showcase things, this fully programmable color LED board is your ideal gadget.

**Adafruit Perma Promo Hat** – This is a basic tool that will allow you to create and test your own custom circuits for use in your projects.

**PaPiRus eink Display Hat** – This is perfect if you are looking for a basic display that isn't going to suck up a bunch of power. This display is great to display a calendar, clock, or thermometer.

**<u>Mini Wireless Keyboard And Mouse Touchpad</u>** – This is great if you don't want to keep your Pi connected to a mouse and keyboard all the time. You aren't going to want to use this when you are typing out long strands of commands. However, it is great if you are only typing a few sudo commands or small mouse movements.

**<u>Cases</u>** – There are many different cases you can get for your Raspberry Pi. From the simplest cases that are used just to protect your Raspberry Pi from the elements, to cases that include a touchscreen holder or even mount to a monitor.

As you can see, there are many different options for accessories for your Raspberry Pi. Most of the accessories you are going to find listed above are available for under one hundred dollars. This means that even if you choose to invest in a few of your favorites, you are still going to be spending less than you would be on a traditional computer, and you are going to be able to do so much more with it.

# *Chapter 28: Sample Project Ideas For Your Raspberry Pi*

Now you know all the technical information about your Raspberry Pi 3 – Model B, as well as some of the basics about using it for programming. From here we are going to go over some sample projects you can do, or build off of, as you begin to learn all that your Raspberry Pi can do.

### Turn Your Raspberry Pi into A Wireless Access Point

There are many different reasons you might want to turn your Raspberry Pi into a wireless access point. Here are some of the most common reasons:

- Extend your existing Wi-Fi Network;

- Learn more about wireless networking;

- Create a free Access Point;

- Build a honey trap to learn about network hardening;

- Learn about sniffing packets;

- Provide guest wireless access that is firewalled through your main network;

- Closed Wi-Fi monitoring station for weather recording, temperature sensing; and

- Create a Raspberry Pi Hot Spot.

The first thing you need to do is ensure that your Raspberry Pi 3 – Model B is all set up and ready to be used. Assuming that it is, you are now going to run **sudo raspi-config** and set up your Pi, changing your memory split to sixteen. You are then going to reboot and set a password, if you choose to, for the root user.

Assuming that you are logged in under Root User, you are now going to install Aptitude with **apt-get install aptitude**. Once this is installed, you are going to use the command **aptitude update; aptitude safe-upgrade**. The speed of your internet is what will determine how long this process is going to take.

Once that has finished, you are going to install a few packages:

**Aptitude install rfkill zd1211-firmware hostapd-utils iw dnsmasq**

These are:

rfkill – Wireless utility

zd1211-firmware – Software for dealing with zd1211 based wireless hardware

hostapd – This is the hostap wireless access point

hostap-utils – These are the tools that go with hostap

iw – Wireless configuration utility

dnsmasq – A DHCP and DNS utility

An addition option is to add **vim** to that list. Vim is a nicer console editor than the default vi.

Next, you are going to locate the file /etc/dhcpcd.conf. Once you have found this file, you are going to add these lines to the end:

**interface wlano**

**static ip_address=192.168.1.1/24**

**static routers=192.168.0.1**

**static domain_name_servers=8.8.8.8 8.8.4.4**

These lines are going to instruct dhcpcd to statically configure the WLANO interface with an IP address. You can change this IP address to whatever you are intending to use for your wireless network. However, you must leave the /24 as it is important and the coding will not work without it. At this time, you should change the gateway from the default 192.168.0.1 to whatever the gateway is on your normal LAN which the wired ETHO interface is connected to. Leave the domain_name_servers as is, that's the Google DNS farm and should always work.

The next thing we are going to do is configure hostap. We are going to edit /etc/hostapd/hostapd.conf to look like this:

**interface=wlano**

**driver=nl80211**

**ssid=test**

**channel=1**

Ensure that you don't leave any spaces at the end of each line, as hostap is very literal in reading its configuration and spaces will alter how the language is being read.

Finally, you are going to configure dnsmasq to allow yourself to obtain an IP address from your new Pi Point. Edit /etc/dnsmasq.conf to look like this:

**# Never forward plain names (without a dot or domain part)**

**domain-needed**

**# Only listen for DHCP on wlan0**

**interface=wlan0**

**# create a domain if you want, comment it out otherwise**

**#domain=Pi-Point.co.uk**

**# Create a dhcp range on your /24 wlan0 network with 12 hour lease time**

**dhcp-range=192.168.1.5,192.168.1.254,255.255.255.0,12h**

**# Send an empty WPAD option. This may be REQUIRED to get windows 7 to behave.**

**#dhcp-option=252,"\n"**

Remember that you are going to change the dhcp-range to match the network IP address you are using. To ensure that your Pi Point is going to work after it is rebooted, you are going to need to create a run file that will turn on forwarding, nat and run hostap at the time of booting. To do this you are going to create a file named /etc/init.d/pipoint with the following contents:

**#!/bin/sh**

**# Configure Wifi Access Point.**

**#**

**### BEGIN INIT INFO**

**# Provides: WifiAP**

**# Required-Start: $remote_fs $syslog $time**

**# Required-Stop: $remote_fs $syslog $time**

**# Should-Start: $network $named slapd autofs ypbind nscd nslcd**

**# Should-Stop: $network $named slapd autofs ypbind nscd nslcd**

# Default-Start: 2

# Default-Stop:

# Short-Description: Wifi Access Point configuration

# Description: Sets forwarding, starts hostap, enables NAT in iptables

### END INIT INFO

# turn on forwarding

echo 1 > /proc/sys/net/ipv4/ip_forward

# enable NAT

iptables -t nat -A POSTROUTING -j MASQUERADE

# start the access point

hostapd -B /etc/hostapd/hostapd.conf

 Next make the script executable with **chmod +x / etc/init.d/pipoint** and add the script to the startup sequence of the Raspberry Pi using **update-rc.d pipoint start 99 2**. This will ensure that your Pi Point will reboot itself as a functioning Wi-Fi access point.


**Turn Your Raspberry Pi 3 – Model B Into A Retro Arcade Machine**

Who doesn't love retro video games? This project is going to show you how to very simply turn your Raspberry Pi into a retro games console in no time.

First, open up a terminal window. You can find this at the top of the screen. Once it's open, type **sudo apt-get update** followed by **sudo apt-get install -y git dialog**. Next, you are going to type **cd** and then **git clone git://github.com/petrockblog/RetroPie-Setup.git**. This is going to download a little script that is going to install tons of game emulators for you. To prepare the installer, type: **cd RetroPie-Setup**, then **chmod +x retropie_setup.sh**.

In the same terminal window, we are going to type: **sudo./retropie_setup.sh**, this is going to run the installer and bring up an awesome retro interface. Once we are here, we are going to select the binaries-based install option. This is going to take about an hour.

Once this is installed, we are going to open up another terminal window and type: **sudo raspi-config**. In this configuration app, you are going to go into the boot options and choose to make the Pi boot into a command prompt instead of Raspbian. Now you are going to reset the Pi, and then type **EmulationStation** to run your new retro game center.

This is going to give you access to emulators for more than twenty systems, including the Mega Drive and Nintendo 64. While some games are going to be built in, you are going to have to check out a site like *emuparadise.*

## Create A Media Center With Your Raspberry Pi

Before you get started on making your Raspberry Pi into a media center, you are going to need to obtain a few components:

- Raspberry Pi Case
- Standard SD card
- Micro-USB cable and wall charger
- HDMI cable
- USB mouse and keyboard

The first thing you are going to do is get your Raspberry Pi set up in the case. The board should fit snugly in the case without needing to be forced in. Once you have placed your Raspberry Pi into your case and screwed the top on, you are ready to move on.

The media center is going to run on RaspBMC Linux distribution, and you are going to need to download this from a computer other than the Raspberry Pi. Once you unzip the file, right click the file **setup.exe** and select "Run as Administrator" click yes to the User Account Control dialog. You will then be presented with an interface which will allow you to install the RaspBMC to an SD card. Next, select the SD card from the list and check the box stating that you agree with the license agreement and select install.

Now that the software has been installed on the SD card, you are going to insert it into the Raspberry Pi. Turn the Raspberry Pi on and begin the installation process. This can take up to forty-five minutes.

Now that RaspBMC has been installed, you are going to be given the option to choose a language, and will then be greeted with the home screen. Scroll over to the program section and select the RaspBMC settings option. This is going to allow you to change your connection type from wired to wireless. You are going to be able to change many other settings to personalize your experience.

Now you are ready to add your media. Since it is impractical to store your media on the SD card, we are going to be streaming the media from an existing computer.

Go to the home menu and navigate to the video option. Here, you should see a drop-down option for files, choose this option and then click the option to add videos. This should give you a menu that allows you to browse for a source.

Select browse. A screen will appear that contains a variety of options to connect. XBMC facilitates a number of different connection options. However, most computers are going to rely on the Windows Samba option, which you will find near the bottom. Once you have clicked on this option, it is going to ask you for the username and password for the computer you are trying to stream from. Enter this information, and you will be able to view the files that you have chosen to share. Now that you have added your media, you should be able to select the media and begin streaming content.

There are three different methods you can use to control the device you have just created.

1 – A wireless mouse is one option, although it is also the most inconvenient.

2 – There are various apps you can get for your Android or iPhone.

3 – A universal remote. This is the most ideal option since you likely already have one of these in your home.

There are many, many more things you can do with your new Raspberry Pi 3 – Model B. We've walked through two of the most popular, and easiest, things you can do. Below is a list of other things that your Raspberry Pi is capable of. Feel free to attempt any of these projects, or create one of your very own, the only limit with the Raspberry Pi is your imagination.

## **Other Raspberry Pi Projects**
- Write your own game
- Make a Gameboy (advanced)
- Make a Kodi streamer
- Build a download hub
- Create a dedicated Minecraft machine
- Build a camera trap
- Build a case for your Raspberry Pi
- Control your stereo wirelessly

- Create your own cloud server

- Make a phone

- Make a PiRate radio station

- Build a smart beer fridge

- Make a PiCam

- Make a talking toy

- Make a bitcoin mining machine

- Create a tiny arcade

- Build your own virtual assistant, similar to Amazon's Alexa

- Build a Raspberry Pi laptop

- Stream PC games to the Pi

- Raspberry Pi music player

- Raspberry Pi photo frame

- Make a motion sensor

- Raspberry Pi security camera network

- Build a Samba server

- Create a smart mirror

As you can see, the options of what you can do with the Raspberry Pi are virtually endless. Choose a project to get started with, and remember, if something ever goes wrong, simply go back to the beginning and reprogram your Raspberry Pi as if it were brand new.

# *Chapter 29: Python Programing – An Overview*

Getting started with a new programming language can be a bit scary. You want to make sure that you are picking out one that is easy to use so that you can understand what is going on inside of the program. But you may also have some big dreams of what you want to accomplish with the programming and want an option that is able to keep up with that. The good news is that the Python programming language is able to help with all of this and is the perfect coding language for a beginner to get started with.

There are many reasons why you would enjoy working with the Python language. It is easy to learn, is meant for beginners, and it works with some of the other coding languages that you may want to learn to add in more power. It is based on the English language so there are not going to be too many issues with learning difficult words, and it has a lot of the power that you need without all the complicated make-up of other coding languages. As you will see in a minute, the syntax in Python is really easy to learn and there are a lot of powerful things that you can do with this coding language, even as a beginner.

The Python library is going to be a great help to you as you get started with this language. It has many of the syntaxes and examples that you need to help you out when you get stuck or when you have some issues figuring out how to complete some steps in Python. The community with this coding language is large as well, due to the fact that this is an easy code to work with and is great for beginners, so you will be able to find others to ask questions of or you can read through forums to learn more about the projects you want to work on.

If you are interested in getting started with the Python language, there are a few things that you will need to have on hand to make the process easier. First, you will need to make sure that the right text editor is in place on your computer. This is important because it is the software that you need to use in order to write out the codes to use inside of Python. The text editor doesn't have to be high end or complicated, and in fact, using the free Notepad option on any Windows computer, or another of this nature, will work just fine.

Once you have chosen the text editor that you would like to use, you will be able to download the actual Python program to use. The nice thing about this is that Python is free to download, as is the IDE and the other options that you will need, so you won't have to worry about the financial aspect of it. To get the Python program set up, you will just need to visit the Python website and choose the version that you would like to use.

While you are getting the Python program set up on your computer, you will also need to make sure that you download the IDE in the same instance. The IDE is basically the environment that you are going to be working in, and it will include the compiler that you need to interpret the codes that you are writing. It is often best to use the one that comes with the Python programming because this one is designed to work the best, but if you are used to working with a different IDE, you will be able to use that one as well.

If you find that there are times that you have questions about using this coding language, such as how to work on a particular code or if you are lost about why something isn't working, you should take the time to visit a Python community. The Python language has been around for some time, and it is one of the most popular coding languages in use, so the communities are pretty large. You should be able to find many groups of beginners and those who are more advanced who will be able to help you with your questions or any of the concerns that you have while learning this language.

## Some of the basic parts of the Python code

Now that you have some of the Python software all set up and ready to go, it is time to work on some of the basics that come with this code. There are a lot of different parts that work together to write some amazing codes inside of Python, but learning about these basics will make it a bit easier to handle and when getting into some of the more complex processes later on. Here are some of the basics that we are going to concentrate on first before moving to some of the harder stuff later on:

*Keywords*

Any coding software that you use is going to have some keywords. These are words that will tell the interpreter what you want to happen in the code, so they are important to be familiar with. It is recommended that you do not use these anywhere else in your code in order to avoid confusion or error when the interpreter gets ahold of it, considering these are major action words. Some of the keywords that you should look at when working in the Python language include:

- False
- Finally
- Class
- Is
- Return
- Continue

- None
- For
- Try
- True
- Lambda
- Def
- Nonlocal
- From
- While
- Global
- Del
- And
- Not
- Raise
- In
- Except
- Break
- Pass
- Yield
- As
- If
- Elif
- Or
- Import
- Assert
- Else
- Import

This is a good list to keep on hand when you are writing your codes. This will help you to send the right information to the interpreter when you are writing through the code. Any time that you see an error message come up after writing out code make sure to check if you used one of those words properly within your statements.

*Names of Identifiers*

While working on a new code or program with Python, you will need to work with a few different things including variables, functions, entities, and classes. These will all have names that are also called identifiers. When you are creating the name of an identifier, regardless of the type you are working on, some of the rules that you should follow include:

- You should have letters, both lower case and upper casework are acceptable, the underscore symbol, and numbers. You are able to choose any combination of these as well. Just make sure that there are no spaces between characters.
- You can never start an identifier with a number. You are able to use something like "sixdogs," but "6dogs" would not be acceptable.
- The identifier should not be one of the keywords that were listed above, and there should never be one of the keywords inside of it.

If you do go against one of these rules, you will notice that a syntax error will occur and the program will close on you. In addition to the rules above, you should ensure that the identifiers are easy to read for the human eye. This is important because while the identifier may follow the rules that were set out above, they can still have trouble when the human eye isn't able to understand what you are writing out.

When you are creating your identifier, make sure that you pick one that will be descriptive. Going with one that will describe what the code is doing or what the variable contains is a good place to start. You should also be wary of using abbreviations because these aren't always universally understood and can cause some confusion.

# *Chapter 30: Basic Commands You Should Know in Python*

In addition to the things that we discussed above pertaining to the Python language, there are some other things that you can put into your codes to make them really strong. There are many options and functions that you can incorporate into the codes in order to do things like: tell other programmers what to do inside the code, add similar parts with the same characteristics together, and so much more. Let's take some time to look at the different commands that you are able to use in your codes with Python and what they all mean.

## Comments

Comments are a great thing to know how to use inside of Python. They allow you to leave little notes inside of the code for yourself or for other coders who want to take a look at what you are doing. The compiler is set up to not recognize these comments, this way you are able to put in as many comments as you would like without it affecting how the code is going to execute.

Python makes it really easy to add in these comments. You will simply need to use the "#" sign in front of the comment that you want to leave inside the code. Once you are done with the comment that you want to leave, you just need to hit the return button and start out on a new line so that the compiler knows that you are starting on a new part of the code. As mentioned, you are able to leave as many of these little notes inside of your code as you would like, but try to keep them just to the ones that are needed in order to keep the code looking nice and organized.

## Statements

Another thing that you are able to add into your code is statements. Whenever you are working on a code, you will need to leave these statements inside of your code so that the compiler has some idea of what you would like to have shown up on the screen. A statement is going to basically be a unit of code that you can send over to the interpreter. Then your interpreter will look at the statement that you want to use and then execute it based on the command that you are giving it.

When you work on writing the code, you can choose how many statements you are able to write at one time. You can choose to just have one statement that is inside of your code, or you can have several of them based on what you would like to have happen inside of the code. As long as you keep the statements inside of the brackets inside the code and you use all the correct rules when you are writing out that part of the code, you will be able to include as many of these statements as needed into the code.

When you choose to add in a statement (or more than one statement) into the code, you will send it through to the interpreter, which is then going to work to execute the commands that you want, just as long as you make sure that you put everything else in the right place. The results of your statements will then show up on the screen when you execute it, and you can always go back in and make changes or adjustments as needed. Let's look at an example of how this would work when using statements in your code:

$x = 56$
*Name = John Doe*
$z = 10$

*print(x)*

*print(Name)*

*print(z)*

When you send this over to the interpreter, the results that should show up on the screen are:

56

John Doe

10

It is as simple as that. Open up Python and give it a try to see how easy it is to just get a few things to show up in your interpreter.

**Working with variables**

Variables are a good thing to learn about the inside of the Python code because they can be used to store your code in specific parts of your computer. So basically, you will find these variables are just spots on the memory of your computer that will be reserved for the values of the code that you are working on. When you are working on the variables in the code, you are telling the computer to save some room on its memory to store these variables. Depending on what type of data you would like to use in the code, the variable is able to tell the computer what space should be saved on that location.

*Giving the variable a value*

In order to make the variables work inside the code, you need to make sure that they get a value assigned to each. Otherwise they are just basic places on the memory. You need to put some kind of value to the variable in order to get it to work properly, so it reacts inside the code. There are two types of variables that you will be able to use, and the one that you choose will determine the value type that you give to it. The different types of variables that we can pick from include:

Float: this would include numbers like 3.14 and so on.

String: this is going to be like a statement where you could write out something like "Thank you for visiting my page!" or another similar phrase.

Whole number: this would be any of the other numbers that you would use that do not have a decimal point.

When you are using this program, you will not need to use declarations in order to reserve this space on the memory since this is something that will occur right when you add a value to the variable you are working with. If you want to make sure that this is going to happen automatically, you just need to use the (=) symbol so that the value knows which variable it is supposed to be working with:

Some examples of how this works include:

*x = 12*          *#this is an example of an integer assignment*

*pi = 3.14*        *#this is an example of a floating point assignment*

*customer name = John Doe*        *#this is an example of a string assignment*

Now at this point, we are looking at just writing the code, but what if you would like to have the interpreter execute the code that we are using. Luckily, this is pretty simple to work on. You just need to make sure that you write out the word "print" before the statement that you want to use. However, in the newer versions, such as Python 3, you would want to add in the parenthesis. Either way, this is pretty easy to learn how to do. Here is a good example of how you would be able to make this work inside Python:

*print(x)*

*print(pi)*

*print(customer name)*

Based on the information listed above, when this is printed out, your interpreter is going to execute the results:

*12*

*3.14*

*John Doe*

You are also able to add in more than one value to the same variable if this is what needs to happen for the code to work within your code. You just need to make sure that you are including the equal sign ("=") in between each of the parts to make it work the right way. For example, "a = b = c = 1" would be acceptable and makes it so that all of those variables would equal 1 inside of your code. This is just a simpler option to use rather than writing each of these out on their own and making them equal to 1.

These are just a few more of the basics that you will need to learn how to use when it comes to writing out your own codes in Python. These are pretty simple to learn how to do and you are going to enjoy all the power that they add into even the simplest codes you will be writing in the beginning.

# *Chapter 31: Working with Loops in Python*

Now that we know some of the basics associated with working on the Python language, it is time to move into some of the more complex parts of this language and learn how to make it all work for your program. With the other options included in this guidebook, we talk about decision control instructions or sequential control instructions. When we are working with the decision control options (which will be discussed in the following chapter), we are putting the calculations into a fixed order to be figured out. With the sequential option, the interpreter is going to execute your instructions based on how your conditions will turn up at the end. There are a few limitations that come up with these options, mostly because they are only able to do the action once.

Now, what happens if you would like to have the action done more than once? With the other options that we discussed in this book, this would mean that you would need to rewrite the code over and over again until it is repeated as many times as you would like it to be. But what happens when you want to make something like a table that counts from 1 to 100? Do you want to write out the same part of code 100 times to make this happen?

Luckily, there are some options within Python that can be used to make it easier to write out these things as many times as you would like, while only taking up a few lines. These are called "loops," and they ensure that you are able to repeat the code as many times as you would like, from one to a thousand or higher if you would like. They are much easier to write out, they can save you a lot of time, and they will basically ensure that you are going to get the loop to continue until the conditions of the code are no longer true.

At first, you may feel that these loops are going to be kind of complicated because you have to tell the program how to repeat itself over and over as many times as you want, but it is actually pretty simple. There are three different types of loops that you can use inside of Python depending on what you would like the code to do. The three loops that you are able to use include the "while" loop, the "for" loop, and the "nesting" loop. Each of the loops is going to work in a different way to help you to repeat the part of the code that you need as many times as needed. Let's take a look at how each of these work, and when you would choose to use each one inside of your code.

## What is the while loop?

The first loop that we are going to take a look at is the while loop. This is a good one to start on when you would like to make the code repeat itself, or go through the same actions, a fixed amount of times. For example, if you want to make sure that the loop goes through the same steps ten times, you would want to use the while loop. But if you would like to use this to create an indefinite number of loops, this is not the option to go with.

One of the examples that you would want to use with the while loop is when calculating out the amount of interest that is owed or paid. You can do this several times in order to find the perfect option for your user, but this one can be set up so that the user will not have to go back through the program multiple times and get frustrated. Here is a good example that you can use in order to learn how the while loop statements are going to work when you would like to calculate simple interest:

*#calculation of simple interest. Ask user to input principal, rate of interest, number of years.*

```
counter = 1
while(counter <= 3):
        principal = int(input("Enter the principal amount:"))
        numberofyeras = int(input("Enter the number of years:"))
        rateofinterest = float(input("Enter the rate of interest:"))
        simpleinterest = principal * numberofyears * rateofinterest/100
        print("Simple interest = %.2f" %simpleinterest)
        #increase the counter by 1
        counter = counter + 1
        print("You have calculated simple interest for 3 time!")
```

With this particular loop, the user will be able to put in the numbers they want to use for interest three times. After they are done, it will be set up to have a message show up on the screen. You can make this more complicated if you would like, adding in more lines for the user to input their answer as many times as they choose. The user of the program will be the one in charge, choosing how much they want to put into each of the spots. The user will be able to redo this program as well, starting over at the beginning, if they would like to add in more than the three interest spots than what they have in right now.

**Working with the for loop**

Now that we understand a bit more about the while loop, it is time to move on to the for loop. This one will work similarly to the other loop, but is a more traditional way to work with loops. If you have worked in any other coding languages in the past, you may be more familiar with this particular loop. If you do plan to use Python with another coding language, you should consider using the for loop to make things easier.

When using the for loop, the user will not be the one who defines the conditions that will make the loop stop. The Python program is going to make the statement continue repeating, in the exact order that it is placed inside your statement. Below you will find an example of how the for loop would work inside your code:

*# Measure some strings:*
*words = ['apple', 'mango', 'banana', 'orange']*
*for w in words:*
*print(w, len(w))*

Take some time to insert these statements into your compiler. With this one, the four fruits that are in this code, or the other statements that you choose to use, will repeat in the order that you write them out. If you are writing out this particular code and you want to make sure that they come out in a different order than what is listed above, you will need to make sure that you turn them around when writing the code. The computer will not take the time to make the changes and it is not going to allow you to change these at all when you are working on the actual code.

On the other hand, if you are looking for the loop to just go through a certain sequence of numbers or words, such as only wanting the first three fruits to show up on the screen, you will find that using your range() function is the best one for this. This function is going to generate a big list of the arithmetic progressions that you can use inside of the code to help make this easier.

**The nested loops**

The third type of loop that we are going to take a look at is the nested loop. This one is going to sound a bit more complicated than you are used to with the other two options, but the code is actually going to be shorter than the others, and all the options that you are going to be able to do with the nested loop can make it a great one to learn even as a beginner. To keep things basic, the nested loop is just a loop that is inside of another loop. Both of the loops will just keep going through the repeat process until both of the programs have time to finish.

We are going to take a moment to look at an example of working on the nested loops. We are going to use the idea of a multiplication table in order to show you how several loops inside your code will be able to bring up a lot of information and you will only need to have a few lines of code to make this happen. The code that we are going to write will make the multiplication table go from 1 up to 10. Here is the example that you are able to use:

*#write a multiplication table from 1 to 10*
*For x in xrange(1, 11):*
　　*For y in xrange(1, 11):*
　　*Print '%d = %d' % (x, y, x\*x)*

When you get the output of this program, it is going to look similar to this:

$1^*1 = 1$
$1^*2 = 2$
$1^*3 = 3$
$1^*4 = 4$
$1^*5 = 5$

This would continue going until you got all the way up to $1^*10 = 2$
Then it would move on to do the table by twos such as this:

$2^*1 = 2$

2*2 = 4

2*3 = 6

For this one, you are going to keep on going until you end up with 10*10 and the answer that goes with this. You will have a complete multiplication table without having to write out the lines that go with each one, which makes this whole process easier to handle. Just look at the code above, there are only four lines (one of which is a comment), and you can get a table that is pretty complete and long. This is just one of the samples of what you are able to do and one of the main reasons that people will choose to go with loops rather than trying to write out all of the lines that they need.

Loops are one of the best things that you can work on when it comes to being inside the Python language. It can simplify the code that you are working on and ensures that you are able to get a lot of stuff done inside the code without having too much information written out and making it look like a mess. Try out a few of these loop options in your code and see what a difference they can make.

# *Chapter 32: Handling Exceptions in Your Code*

There are times when you will need to work with exceptions when working inside the code. These can work one of two ways. For the first one, it is an exception that the program doesn't like, such as trying to divide a number by zero. When this happens, an error is going to come up on the screen, but you will be able to change the message that comes up on the screen with this to help avoid issues and to make sure that your user has some idea of what the issue is. Then there are exceptions that are particular to your program. If you do not want to allow your user to put in a certain number or another input, you would want to raise an exception to make this not allowed.

So any time that you would like to show the user that a condition is considered abnormal within the code, you will want to bring out the exceptions. There are several types of these that show up inside of the code, and some of which are as simple as writing out the code the wrong way or using the incorrect spelling that will cause the errors.

Any time that you are working in your Python program, and you want to make sure that you are bringing up the exceptions in the proper way, you will want to check out the Python library. There are several of these exceptions that are already in place inside the library and will save you a lot of time. It can be extremely beneficial when you check these exceptions out first. There are several exception types that you are able to use inside this language, including whenever you are dividing a number by zero, or whenever you try to reach a part that is outside the end of the file.

Exceptions can be a nice thing to work with within Python. The nice thing is that you aren't stuck dealing with the error messages that come up on a code. You can change them up a bit to help explain what is going on to the user so that any confusion can be bypassed. When an error message comes up on the screen, it can be difficult to determine what is wrong, especially if your user has no experience working with coding at all. But when you can make some changes, such as adding in a message like "you are trying to divide by zero!" it can explain what is going on with the error so the user can correct or change their process, and makes your code a bit more user-friendly.

You are also able to make some of your own exceptions if the code you are writing asks for it. You will not be able to find these inside of the Python library, but it is still an option that you are able to use. You will need to create some of these on your own so that an error, which can be a message like you did with the ones that were found in the library, will make things easier for the user to understand why the error is showing up.

When you are trying to write out exceptions within the Python language, there are a few things that you are going to find inside of your Python library in which you should take a bit of time to look over and learn how to work with. If you would like to work on the exceptions, you will need to make sure that you learn some of the key terms that need to be present to tell the compiler what you are doing. There are many options to choose from, but some of the statements that are best for working inside of your code with exceptions inside of Python coding include:

- Finally: with this one, you will be able to bring up the word to do the cleanup actions. This is a good one to use whether the user brings up the exception or not.
- Assert: this is the condition that is used whenever you would like to trigger that an exception has occurred inside the code.

- Try/except: these are the keywords that you will want to use whenever you are trying out a block of code. It is going to be recovered because of the exception that was raised either by you or by the Python program for some other reason.

- Raise: when you use the raise command, you are working to trigger the exception outside the code, doing so manually.

These are some of the best words to use in order to work with your exceptions and to make sure also that you will get all of your errors and other parts to work within the code. Whether you want to raise an exception that is recognized by the code or you are trying to work with one that is just for your program, in particular, you will be able to use these to help make things work within the code.

**Raising an exception**

Now that we have taken some time to look at what exceptions are all about, it is now time to learn how to raise exceptions. This is a pretty easy concept for you to work on and understand. For example, whenever you are working with the code inside of Python, and there is some kind of issue that is coming up with it, or you see that the program is trying to do things that aren't allowed within the rules of Python, the compiler is going to raise an exception for the behavior in question. This is because the program is going to see the issue and will not be sure about how it should react.

In some cases, the exception that is going to be raised will be pretty simple and could be something like naming the code the wrong way or spelling something wrong. You will just need to go back through the code and make the changes. Or there could even be some issues with the user attempting an action that is not allowed by the code, such as when a user may try to divide by zero. Let's take a look at how this is going to work so that you can see the steps that are needed in order to raise an exception:

*x = 10*

*y = 10*

*result = x/y #trying to divide by zero*

*print(result)*

The output that you are going to get when you try to get the interpreter to go through this code would be:

*>>>*

*Traceback (most recent call last):*

   *File "D: \Python34\tt.py", line 3, in <module>*

   *result = x/y*

*ZeroDivisionError: division by zero*

*>>>*

For the example that we did above, the Python coding language is going to show an error because you were trying to take a number and divide it by zero. The Python language is one that won't allow you to do this action, and so the error is going to come up on the screen. As we mentioned above, when you see that this error is coming up, the user may be confused and not understand what is going on at all. When you use this to raise up an exception, you should consider changing up the message so that the user has some idea of what is going on so that he or she can make the correct and necessary changes so that the code will work the way that it should.

## How to make your own exceptions

So far, we have spent most of our time looking at the steps that you will need to take in order to work with the exceptions that are already recognized by the system. But what happens when you would like to raise some of your own exceptions that work with your particular program that the system does not already recognize? A good example for this is when you want to make sure that your user is not able to place specific numbers into the system. You want to make sure that when the user places these numbers into the system, they are going to get an exception. Or if you would like the user to put in five numbers and they only put in four, you could use the idea of exceptions as well.

The trick with this type of action is that the Python program may not see that there is even an issue. The program is not going to realize that there is an issue with just putting in four numbers rather than the five unless you tell it that this is an issue. You will be the one who is able to set up the exceptions that you want to use, and you can mess around and add in any exception that you would like as long as it meets up with the other rules that are used inside of Python. Let's take a look at the example that is below so that we can understand how the exceptions work and to get some practice with using these:

```python
class CustomException(Exception):
def_init_(self, value):
        self.parameter = value
def_str_(self):
        return repr(self.parameter)


try:
        raise CustomException("This is a CustomError!")
except CustomException as ex:
```

*print("Caught:", ex.parameter)*

When you use this syntax, you will get the message of "Caught: This is a CustomError!" and any time that your user is on the program and puts in the wrong information, the error message is going to show up. This error is going to be caught if you put the conditions into the program the right way and it is important, especially if you set up your own exceptions in the code, that you place the conditions into the code.

It is possible to add in any wording as you would like into this part, so you can change it up as much as you would like to help better explain to the user what the error message means or what they may be doing wrong.. Mess around with this a little bit and you will find that it is easier than ever to set up some of your own exceptions or deal with the exceptions that are going on inside of your code.

Working with exceptions is a great way to ensure that you are getting the most out of your code. There are times when the code will see an abnormal condition and will need to put up a message or you will be working on your own program, and you will want to make up some of these abnormal conditions to work with what you are doing. Take a look at some of the examples that are done inside of this chapter, and you will be able to work with any of the exceptions that you would like in Python.

# *Chapter 33: Conditional Statements in Python*

When it comes to working with your code, there will be times when you will want to make sure that the code is going to function in a specific way based on the conditions that you set, as well as the answer that the user puts in. You can keep it simple and have only one answer as an output when the user inputs an answer that is considered true based on your conditions, or you can make it more complex so that different answers will come up based on whether the input from the user is true or false. You can also give the user multiple options to input, and they can choose from those. In this chapter, we are going to take some time to talk about the different conditional statements that will work inside the Python code, including the "if" statement, the "if else" statement and the "elif" statements.

**The if statement**

The first statement that we are going to work with inside of Python is the "if" statement. This is the most basic of the conditional statements, and it is often a good place to start when first learning code. But there will be some challenges when it comes to the user putting in an answer that does not agree with the conditions you set.

With the if statement, you must set the conditions and then the program will do the rest, waiting for the answer from the user. If the user puts in an answer that is considered true, based on the conditions that you set, the rest of the code will be executed. This is usually in the form of a statement of some sort showing up on the screen, and then the compiler moving on to the next part of the code. On the other hand, if the user puts in an answer that is not allowed or is considered false based on the conditions that you set, nothing is going to happen. The if statements are not set up for false answers, so the program will just stop at that point.

There are going to be some issues with this of course, but it is a good place to get started. This one will help you to see how the conditional statements are going to work and gets you some practice with the compiler, but we will look at some conditional statements that are able to look further into the work we are doing so that answers will show up regardless of the answers that are put in. Let's take a look at an example of working with the if statement to give you some practice.

*age = int(input("Enter your age:"))*
*if (age <=18):*

   *print("You are not eligible for voting, try next election!")*
*print("Program ends")*

Let's take a look at this syntax a bit to see what is going on. With this one, when the user comes onto the site and says that their age is under 18, they will match as true with the conditions that you set. This means that the statement that you put in, the "You are not eligible for voting, try next election!", will come up on the screen.

On the other hand, if the user puts in that they are another age, such as 25, into this code, nothing is going to happen. The if statement is not set up in order to handle this issue and there are no statements that are going to show up if this situation occurs. The compiler will just stop working on the code because it is false. You will need to make some changes to the code to handle this.

For the most part, you are not going to be able to use this type of conditional statement. The user is not wrong if they enter an age that is above 18 in the example above and they aren't going to really care for it if they can't see any results after they enter their age. How would you feel if you put in an answer to a program and it just stopped? The if statement is not the most efficient method of taking care of your conditional statements, so there will be many times that you should avoid using this at all. That is where the if else statement is going to come in handy.

## If else statement

As we talked about above, there are some issues that come up when using the if statement. If your user enters an answer that is considered true with the if statement, the correct part of the code will execute. But if your user enters an answer that is seen as false (even if it is true for them), they will end up with a blank screen. This can easily end up with some problems when working within your code.

This is when the if else statement is going to come in use. With this one, you are able to set up true and false conditions, and different parts of the code are going to be executed based on the answers that the user gives. Pertaining to the prior example, the user could receive an answer saying they are not able to vote if they say they are under 18. But if they input an answer of 30, they would get a second answer, such as information on their closest voting poll or another relevant piece of information.

The if else statement is going to allow for more freedom inside of your code. This makes it easier than ever before for you to handle whatever answer the user puts into the system, whether it is considered true or false. With this statement, the compiler will check the answer, and if it is seen as true for that particular one, it will execute that part of the code. But if not, it moves on to the second part of the code and executes that. You are able to expand on this, going down as many times as you would like if you want to have several different answers. Here is a good example of how you would be able to use the if else statement inside of Python:

*age = int(input("Enter your age:"))*

*if (age <=18):*

    *print("You are not eligible for voting, try next election!")*

*else*

    *print("Congratulations! You are eligible to vote. Check out your local polling station to find out more information!)*

*print("Program ends")*


With this example above, there are basically two options that you can use in the statement. If the user puts in their age as being 18 or younger, the first statement is the one that is going to come up. So on the screen, they are going to see the message "You are not eligible for voting, try next election!" But if the user puts in that they are 19 or above in age, they will see a different message that says: "Congratulations! You are eligible to vote. Check out your local polling station to find out more information!". This is a simple example that shows how the user will be able to put in any age that they want and the answer corresponding to their specific input is going to show up on the screen.

This one is a basic version of what you are able to do with the if else statement. This one just has one true, and one false answer and that is all that is on the statement. But there are times when you would like to have some options that the user can choose from, or you want there to be more than one true answer. For example, let's say that you would like to have the user put their favorite color. You could have five of the else statements with blue, red, yellow, green, and white. If the user puts in one of those five colors, the statement that is with that color will come up. Add in a break part that will catch all the other colors that your user may want to pick from so that an answer comes up no matter what answer they pick out.

The if else statements are able to add a lot of great things that you can use with your codes. It allows it to make a decision inside of the code based on the conditions that you set and the input that your user places into the code. It is nice to use the if else statements because you can better prepare for the various answers that your user will enter, no matter what they decide to answer, and you are all set to go.

## The elif statements

One more conditional statement that we are going to talk about in this chapter is the elif statement. These are a bit different than the others, but they are nice to work with because they provide the user with a few choices that they can choose from. Each of your choices are going to have a statement or a part of the code that will execute based on the decision that your user decides to go with. If you are creating a game and would like to make sure that the user can pick from several options before going further on, the elif statement is the one that you should use. The syntax that you would want to use with the elif statement includes:

*if expression1:*
*statement(s)*
*elif expression2:*
*statement(s)*
*elif expression3:*
*statement(s)*
*else:*
*statement(s)*

This is the basic syntax that you will want to work with whenever you want to use the elif statements in Python. You can just add in some of the information that you want so that the user can see the choices and pick the numbers that they would like to go with it, or the statements that work with their choices. This is one that you will be able to expand out a bit as you need, and you can choose to have two or three options or twenty options based on what you would like to see happen with the elif statements.

Here, we are going to take some time to look at how the elif statement is able to work in your coding. With this option, we are going to list a few choices of pizzas that the user is able to pick from and the corresponding number that they are able to work with. You can always add in some more options as well, and we add in an else part that is able to catch all the other options or, in this option, that will allow them to get a drink instead of a pizza if they do not like the options that are presented to them. Let's take a look at how this would be written out in your Python compiler:

```
Print("Let's enjoy a Pizza! Ok, let's go inside Pizzahut!")
print("Waiter, Please select Pizza of your choice from the menu")
pizzachoice = int(input("Please enter your choice of Pizza:"))
if pizzachoice == 1:
        print('I want to enjoy a pizza napoletana')
elif pizzachoice == 2:
        print('I want to enjoy a pizza rustica')
elif pizzachoice == 3:
        print('I want to enjoy a pizza capricciosa')
else:
        print("Sorry, I do not want any of the listed pizza's, please bring a Coca Cola for me.")
```

This is a pretty simple example of the elif statement and how you would be able to incorporate it into your codes. You can easily change this up to work with whatever program or game that you would like to create. The syntax, as you can see above, is offering the user a few options of pizzas that they are able to choose. When they are using the code, they will be able to pick the number that they would like and that corresponds to the pizza they want to go with. For example, if they would like to get the pizza napoletana, they would type in the number one. If they pick number one, they would see the answer "I want to enjoy a pizza napoletana" come up on their screen. This works for any of the numbers that they would choose on this option. With this one, we have even set it up so that the user can choose to just have a drink without a pizza if this is what they prefer.

The if statements are one of the best options for you to work with. They allow the code to come up with its own decisions based on the conditions that you set up in the beginning. You can make it as simple as the code just choosing to show a result when the user input is the same as your conditions, or you can add in some other parts to match up with the answers that the user places inside the code or with the choices that they want to make. There are many things that you are able to work with when using the conditional statements and you can make them as complicated or as simple as you would like.

Printed in Great Britain
by Amazon